REAL-WORLD SURVIVAL!
What Has Worked For Me

By Walt Rauch

RAUCH & COMPANY, LTD.
Lafayette Hill, PA 19444

Photographs on the following pages by Josh Markowitz:

Pages 7, 54 (bottom photo), 55, 56, 59, 60, 62 (top photo), 65, 66, 68, 69, 71, 73, 74, 87, 88, 130, 131 (top photo), 132 and 144

Library of Congress Catalog Card Number: 98-91247

ISBN 0-9663260-0-8

Layout and Design by Detrich Design

Published by:
RAUCH & COMPANY, LTD.
Lafayette Hill, PA 19444

Printed in the United States of America

To Kathie, my wife, without whom I would not have survived. She is my life and my survival.

ACKNOWLEDGEMENTS

Over the span of a lifetime, there have been many individuals who have taught me and helped me to understand and survive while attending the "school of arms."

I would like to acknowledge everyone who has shared some part of their life experiences and knowledge with me or supported me in difficult times, but the list would be very long and I would invariably forget to mention someone. The following are just some of those who are (or were) men to "ride the river with."

The late Robert John Connolly; J. Woodrow Mathews, Jr.; Harry G. Barbour; the late Peter J. Seitz; Everett Spear; Special Agent-in-Charge (Chief Warrant Officer) Sheldon Goodrich and Special Agent (Sgt-E-7) Robert Arnold, Intelligence Corps, US Army; Special Agent-In-Charge George V. Mesaros and Special Agent Eugene P. Heller, US Secret Service; and Steven T. Horner, Roger D. Tucker, John Lysak, Joseph P. Bunczk, Robert Thomsen, Christopher W. White and Joseph M. Venezia.

The author's Smith & Wesson Model 19 .357 Magnum with 4" barrel, along with some of his Secret Service memorabilia.

TABLE OF CONTENTS

FOREWORD
By Massad Ayoob

I've known the author of the book you're holding for going on twenty years. We met during post-shooting revels at the 1980 Bianchi Cup, where I promptly spilled a beer on him. Walt could tell the story better.

Indeed, Walt could tell *most* stories better. He's the best raconteur in the firearms world since Skeeter Skelton. Rauch has been a lot of places — from the US Secret Service to the Philadelphia Warrant Squad to high risk investigation — and done a lot of things. When he talks of home security, for example, listen to him: Walt Rauch was the "legal burglar" I wrote of in my book, *"The Truth About Self Protection,"* who learned by experience when, empowered by warrants issued by judges, he broke into the homes of felons he'd come to arrest.

I told Walt the night I met him that he ought to write a book. After 17 years, he finally did. I'm obviously not a persuasive guy.

This is a damn good book. My only complaint with it is, I wanted the author to put in more of his personal experiences. But Walt Rauch shares something else with the late, great Sheriff Skelton: he doesn't like to publish his war stories. A collection of Skelton's readings would indicate that he'd never had to kill a man. That wasn't the case. Skeeter told me privately that he just didn't like having to do it, and didn't like to talk about it. After Skelton's death, I learned of a bank robbery in which a local cop had emptied his .38 into a shotgun-armed thug, who kept on coming. Skeeter saved that eternally-grateful cop's life with a single, perfectly-placed (and fatal) bullet

11

from his Smith & Wesson .44 Special. This may explain why Skelton never had much use for .38s except as back-up. But for Skelton, it sufficed to publish the distilled advice that came from his experiences, and not the experiences themselves.

In *"Real-World Survival!,"* Walt Rauch has taken a similar path. Rather than talk of his own armed encounters, Walt has focused on sharing the lessons distilled from those experiences...lessons of guns and of tactics and of lifestyles, but especially of attitude and mental preparation. He warns you up front that everything that worked for him won't necessarily work for you. That's the honest truth. It's a case of "You say to-*may*-to and I say to-*mah*-to." Walt says "destroy" and I say "neutralize."

But a surprisingly huge amount of what you're going to read will work for anyone. Human violence is human violence. Whether you're large or small, male or female, veteran or novice, you're going to face the exact same perpetrator and you'll have to deal with him in almost exactly the same way if you want to survive to go home to your family.

Rauch *did* survive to go home to his family and there are lessons there, too. He's an adoring husband to his bright and beautiful wife, Kathie. I've enjoyed watching him with his fine son, young Walt. As a father, Rauch seemed part stern, part permissive and all understanding, the same traits that, not coincidentally, make him a fine instructor. The lesson is, you don't have to be callous to be a survivor. Love, compassion and family values are all part of the formula that makes a survivor, as important as other components like loyalty, righteousness and resolve. Without those things, you soon burn out and realize you have nothing to survive *for.*

Walt Rauch is a tough old bird and a wise man. I've learned a lot from him over the years. And now, as you turn this page and begin, you're going to do what I've been doing since 1980.

You, too, are going to learn a lot from Walt Rauch.

INTRODUCTION

I've written this book so that others may benefit from the results of a lifetime of experiences that I've had, been involved in and seen while dealing with the "bad guys." I'll show you how I've interpreted "mindset" and what guns and gear work for me.

No one book will cover every "trick" you might want to know; a good "Trigger-Nometry" library is a must. I recommend the following books and authors for further serious study. Some of them conflict with others, but in the main, they are singing from the same sheet of music, though perhaps in different keys.

The best of them, *Kill or Get Killed* by Colonel Rex Applegate, is a classic on exactly what the title says. *No Second Place Winner* by the late Bill Jordan succinctly sums up his extensive experience with his set of "bad guys." Both speak to the central issue of survival.

Ed McGivern's seminal work, *Fast and Fancy Revolver Shooting*, pays more attention to the "how" of shooting than the why, as does Bob Nichols' *Secrets of Double Action Shooting*, out of print but worth the work to find if you are at all interested in good revolver techniques.

Elmer Keith's *Sixguns* and *Hell, I Was There* are both good reads and informative, too.

Jeff Cooper is the father of modern defensive handgunning. His principles of gun handling will work for almost everyone and he has captured a great method to teach and explain mindset (although he could have gone much further with the matter).

Massad Ayoob has probably written something on every handgun and technique ever used, excluding the art of dueling. His ability to gather, analyze, experiment, distill and teach the results of his efforts both in classes and through his many books make him a must-read for anyone interested in self-defense with or without a firearm. Jim Cirillo and John Farnum have also written informative books on self-defense.

None of them have all the answers and, by and large, they don't claim that they do. For the most part, the best of the modern teachers refer to themselves as students of the craft, not prophets.

I would hope that my observations, experiences and conclusions might also contribute to the warrior's lexicon of reference material. You will have to decide if the information is of any value to you. My approach works for me. Some of it may help you. A "one-size-fits-all" hat really doesn't fit everyone. Read all these men, then pick and choose those ideas and techniques that fit your particular personality and needs and discard any that don't quite fit you. Survival is very personal. Judge and use that which is best for **you**, not the other guy.

CHAPTER 1

STATE OF MIND

D o you fear death? Do you fear serious bodily injury? Every survival and every winning technique flows from the individual's state of mind. Central to every description of "mindset" is a variation of the will to survive or to win. Surviving or winning means not giving up, but even more important is the determination to **overcome**. A primary facet of mindset is controlling your fears or negating them so that they do not inhibit or restrict your actions, which should be to **destroy**, not "stop" the other guy.

There have been loads of books written on "mindset," but precious little on how one gets there. The state of mind all the writers and advisors are trying to explain is quite simple: *you must no longer fear death or injury.* Then, you can respond *instantaneously* to the attack.

Whoa, you say. This guy is around the bend. That's not a rational way of living. Not fearing death or injury is pathological, you say, and slam this book down. Well, wait just a minute. You started this read to find out what works for me and what might work for you. Is your mind open or closed?

The Samurai and other great warriors learned not to anticipate the joy of victory, the shame of defeat or to fear death and thus were very effective in combat. They joined in battle in a restful state of mind — prepared, attentive and indifferent to the demands they faced. Some religious warriors addressed death by embracing the belief of a better afterlife based on their actions in battle. Whatever the means used, the effect was the same. The threat of death was neutralized, accepted or looked forward to as a reward of battle. Modern warriors must learn this "fear control" to survive and win.

Battle-hardened soldiers inevitably come to accept death as one of the curses of war.

Your opponent, in large battles or individual confrontations, has only one final trump card to play against you — taking your life. His lesser card is maiming or seriously injuring you. You hold the same cards.

After admitting your fears examine them, visualize them, come to know them and come to terms with them. The known fear is a lesser fear and the longer and better you understand your fears the more they diminish, until they are of no real consequence and will have no adverse impact on your actions.

Pause for a moment and consider that most soldiers, before entering battle, make peace with themselves and their world. Some via the church and minister of their choice, some by pouring out their thoughts through letters to loved ones. Others will deliberately give away their most cherished possessions to their comrades. They are all, in one form or another, letting go of those things that bind them to the material world, those ties which enhance the fear of death.

How does this translate to everyday life and the chance confrontation that might develop for a civilian? Or the much more real possibility of a confrontation arising for those who have chosen to carry a "sword" in modern society?

There are a couple of ways that fear can be controlled. One is by repeated exposure to dangerous situations, a very effective means of numbing the stabbing fear that shoots through us before and during a fight. Of course, the downside is that you might not live through the first exposure. All the top race car drivers have had a few wrecks. None have won without crashing sometime and being able to come back to win again. You're the one who has to decide if being the best is worth the price.

When I worked as an investigator on the Philadelphia waterfront, a large part of the job was to stop and search stevedores and other employees and their vehicles as they left the piers. We did this in pairs — two men, no radios, no backup — with only the authority of a civilian investigative agency and some posted signs notifying everyone of our right to search.

The author got to practice numerous survival techniques while working as an investigator on the Philadelphia waterfront.

A waterfront warehouse offers endless hiding places in which a predator can lie in wait for his victim. Being fearful in such surroundings is natural, but one must come to terms with that fear to survive.

My partner and I would stop one man leaving a shipping terminal gate, or on the piers that were two to four city blocks long, jutting out into the river. Often, when we found that he had stolen cargo, we would suddenly be surrounded by anywhere from two to two hundred of his hostile co-workers. You quickly learned to manage confrontations and deal with group hostility and the very real possibility of death or you didn't have a job. I needed the work, so I learned. I would (and did) do whatever was necessary to get the job done. Yes, of course the crowd menaced us in these circumstances, but in this clash of wills, they didn't want to pay the price to "win"!

Now, I'm not advocating a "John Wayne" approach to danger. Charging into a burning building with buckets of gasoline in both hands is suicidal, not heroic. But if the building is burning, there's nothing wrong with learning just how far you can go forward without major damage, sort of like testing ice on a pond. When the ice starts to creak and begins to fracture, you know that you have pushed forward as far as is reasonable.

Second, you do need to take some risks. You don't learn to sail in a storm from the safety of the harbor. I realize that this concept is contrary to most all the current officer survival teachings and civilian self-defense tactics. I'm telling you what has worked for me. It's your call.

I know for instance, to continue the race car driver analogy, that you don't learn how fast you can take a curve without actually going out of control. And I don't believe you can understand and dominate a confrontation or a lethal encounter without either being in the problem or working very close to the edge of the actual situation. So you must practice at or near "reality." Another way to understand fear is by sky diving, white water rafting, mountain climbing, cave exploration — any activity with a large element of risk. In all of these endeavors, you must learn to control and direct your fears in order to succeed.

Here are the nuts and bolts of what I'm talking about. Suppose you have to go through a bad area to get from point A to point B. You hurry through, doors locked, windows up, driving too fast and jumping the lights. You're seeing goblins at every turn. You're frightened and are showing your fear to anyone who might be watching your actions.

Consider this: you're scared in this environment, but there are literally hundreds of other humans who *live* in this same area that is terrifying you. How do they survive daily? They can't just scurry through; they live there. What do they do to live without becoming victims? Obviously, not everyone in the "bad" neighborhood will be a victim. Some, of course, are the predators. But again, they aren't preying on each other, for the most part. Some, I will admit, are sheep, meant only to be shorn.

The ones who are not victims have come to terms with their locality and have adopted a mindset in which they will violently defend themselves and counterattack any-one who threatens them. This attitude projects from them and the predator, "reading" this, normally avoids that person. Of course, there can be legal repercussions to violent actions, even though justified. Our laws are the civilizer of the mob, but *your* position in regard to those laws needs to be understood, acknowledged and factored into any equations of your actions.

The law and its penalties should not dictate that you sur-render or remain in a state of fear, however. If this occurs, then the law will have only the predator to pun-ish; you will be dead. Despite what others have told you, there really isn't any free lunch. You are accountable for your actions if taken before a court of law. Better the court of law than the homicide investigation regarding your demise, however.

Either you choose to live on your feet or your knees. It's still a free country — although those freedoms seem to be dwindling daily. I would add one observation, though. Often it is not possible to make sheep into anything more. Some are born to be eaten. This is a cold fact of life. There are, generally speaking, three types of humans: victims, predators and prickly men. The modern warrior is the latter, *prickly*. He doesn't seek out others to prey on them, nor does he submit to their demands. He acts when he determines that it is morally just and then does so in a decisive manner without any sophomoric remorse. One doesn't cry over destroying a rabid dog. Nor do you have any post-traumatic episodes when having done so.

In the actual confrontation, you must approach, enter into and continue the battle with an empty mind. Not brain dead, just *empty*, with no thoughts of what is going to happen, what is happening or what just happened. You must operate in a total state of the present time.

Another way to explain this is to imagine eating dinner. You don't consciously think about putting the fork to your mouth or swallowing the food. You let your mind do what you have trained it to do without interference. This is how you fight when "fight" is the only option. This is how your weapons must be used, whatever those weapons may be.

One more item to put on your plate. When facing a threat, I've found that the one thought in my mind is that the aggressor *is already dead*. That's correct. If you're facing the bad guy, consider that he's a corpse which just happens to still be erect. He, not you, determines his fate. He is the one acting in such a manner as to cause extreme damage or death to himself. You are merely reacting to his actions. This is not a rationalization of your actions, by any means. But it does transfer the responsibility, properly, to your opponent; a fresh way of approaching a very old problem.

This is also the only chance you have to beat the truism that "action is faster than reaction." If you react without conscious thought with a pre-programmed response, you might just survive. Let's use weapon retention as an example. If you pre-program yourself to take the appropriate countermeasures to anyone grabbing for your holstered handgun, you can effectively block the attack most of the time. But if you stop to think, "Damn, he's trying to grab my gun...what should I do?", the gun will be gone before you act.

This pre-programming must be done judiciously, though. What appears at first to be a gun grab or a life-threatening act may be no more than an innocent move in your direction, so you do need to consider just how "tight" you want to wind your self-defense reactions. You may need to take a split-second to assess the situation.

To sum up, **mindset** is controlling fear, accepting the consequences of your actions and letting yourself perform to the best of your trained ability without the overriding controls of your conscious mind. Certainly a full plate for anyone and not easily achieved. Some of you may decide this is no way to live. Fine. Just as long as you've made an informed choice.

One last bit of advice: If you are to experience any emotion, let it be that of a strong, cold anger for your opponent. He has chosen to take life from you and that cannot be permitted in a moral world. This anger or even rage, if controlled, will get all your physical defense systems up and running at maximum output — all the better to defeat your adversary.

You may well over-adrenalize before, during and after a confrontation. You can experience almost uncontrollable shakes or profuse sweating. Some have violent stomach upsets at the very least. At worst, your bowels will empty. These physical symptoms can be viewed as fear or anger; either emotion will create the same effect. (Actually, your body is preparing itself for battle the best way it can.) Ignore these symptoms as much as possible and use the good side of the reactions to your advantage.

You will probably become very ill-at-ease if you have never experienced the emotion of real anger, for most of us have been properly taught to be ladies and gentlemen and control our passions. In the grips of strong emotions, you may well learn some things about yourself that you may have preferred not to know or to revisit. Again, it's your choice to learn or avoid this mindset.

Which brings us to the question of how might this mind-set be practiced? There's no easy way nor a quick answer. Soldiers exposed to combat develop it, others in high-risk professions have it, certainly those who have survived even a single armed encounter may have developed these abilities. The downside to developing this mindset is somewhat like learning to climb a mountain. You might fall off the mountain and you might fail at the encounters. Not all fights are winnable, even though the fight must be joined.

I really haven't found the best way to "teach" the proper mindset. I can explain it, encourage experimentation, help those who have already been exposed to a conflict to better understand their emotions, thoughts and reactions. Unfortunately, living through a conflict is still the best teacher. I believe that the individual can, once he understands what has transpired under the weight of the conflict, better handle those same feelings and reactions the next time. Be aware, though, that surviving one confrontation doesn't make you "qualified." It is said that a soldier is not a combat veteran until he has survived five battles.

I suggest that, if at all possible, you avail yourself of a knowledgeable guide while attempting to learn fear management; this is no place for amateurs. The penalty for a mistake is absolutely final. Finding such a guide can present a problem, however, for those good men who have "seen the elephant" are not all that ready to relive or share their experiences. Fortunately, men such as Clint Smith of Thunder Ranch and Jim Cirillo, formerly of the NYPD Stakeout Squad, have accepted the responsibility to teach what they have lived (as did the late Bill Jordan, Retired US Border Patrol).There are others, of course, but these men are good benchmarks against which to measure all the others.

The clash of arms — avoid it if you can. But, once begun, enter into it with all the ferocity you possess!

CHAPTER 2

KNOW THE ENEMY

It's all well and good to suggest a certain mindset or posture that is supposed to help you get through a confrontation, but if you don't know who or what the aggressor is, you'll lose the fight, for you'll never see him coming.

You need to fully know and understand your enemy. Let me perform the introduction. Meet "**Otherhuman.**" This guy is not your next door neighbor, your lodge brother, your golfing buddy or fellow church member. Although he is a member of the human race, he doesn't share **any** of the same moral values that you hold. He has no qualms about his actions in rape, robbery, murder or any other action that is devastating to you. He is not easily frightened, if at all, or deterred from his goals.

He understands violence very well, for it is one of his predatory survival tools. He is goal-oriented and will not desist in his actions unless the cost appears to be prohibitive. He is willing to accept some physical damage to himself and, if in a group, accept some casualties as a cost of doing business. Heartwarming fellow, isn't he? It would be a disservice to call him an enemy or a wild animal. Both of these types have some basic values. Otherhuman is far worse!

For example, I had an informant working for me when I

was a Special Agent in the US Secret Service who fit the description of Otherhuman to a "T." He had served 19 ½ years of a 20-year prison sentence in solitary confinement because he was too dangerous to live among the other prisoners. When he got out, he became an informant to earn some money. He also robbed people in his own neighborhood, including drug dealers working nearby. His technique was to go up against them with a sawed-off, double-barrel shotgun and shoot whenever anyone hesitated to give in to his demands.

When I met with him, I got the definite impression that he would most willingly rob or kill me (for my money or maybe just for fun) if he got the chance. I was barely comfortable talking to him with a gun in my hand and another Agent along as backup. In retrospect, I would say he was criminally insane, but there he was, living in your world and mine — for six months, anyway. Then the dope dealers and his neighbors got together and blew him away with shotguns!

I paint this very bleak picture of your potential opponent(s) so that you will start to have some idea of what you're going to be up against when in conflict with him. He neither understands nor shows any mercy, kindness or compassion. As I said before, he is not easily — if at all — frightened by your actions and you can't reason with him.

Otherhuman is the worst of predators. He attacks those whom he perceives as weaker or more vulnerable than he and desists from an attack when he perceives strength and/or lack of fear. This, of course, is not an absolute. Extreme circumstances such as starvation or disease will drive him to desperate measures, thus you must be able to defend yourself.

Most civilized society presupposes some degree of kindness and mercy from their fellow man. Otherhuman has none. You cannot superimpose your values on him, for he won't give you a break, won't let up because of your entreaties, won't stop his actions because you're a nice person. None of this matters. You're part of the food chain to him and he's going to get what he needs from you regardless of the cost to you. He thinks in very simple terms. You have what he wants and he's going to take it, period.

This must be completely understood and accepted by you if you are going to survive. *No normal societal interactions work.* You must meet Otherhuman on his terms and defeat him. Doubts, hesitations and uncertainty are all his tools, provided by you to be used by him against you. He has made a life study of you. How much time have you spent looking at him?

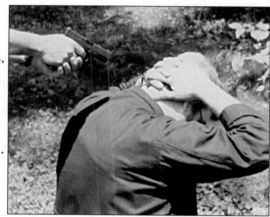

You must out-think and out-fight Otherhuman...for you will be shown no mercy.

In case you're sitting there right now saying to yourself, "Nah, the bad guys can't be that bad!," permit me to pass along a few quotes from an article that ran in *The Philadelphia Inquirer* newspaper on Sunday, December 6, 1992 entitled "A New Generation of Killers, Feeling No Blame and No Shame." It was written by Inquirer Staff Writer Dianna Marder and its contents are positively chilling.

According to Marder, the Inquirer reviewed 57 cases of *teenagers* charged with murder and conducted in-depth interviews with 18 of the youths. They found that "virtually every one sees himself as not responsible for the murder...as not violent," and "certainly not a killer." In fact, these teenage killers said that a single murder is "no big deal." In the article, James Alan Fox, Dean of the College of Criminal Justice at Northeastern University in Boston, makes the point that "this generation of youth has a more casual attitude toward human life." He has dubbed them "the young and the ruthless."

In essence, when Otherhuman enters your world, attacks you or yours, you must destroy him immediately. Failure to act with finality will only result in your death or the death of your loved ones. Otherhuman will not hesitate in his goal; be resolute in yours.

Am I advocating murder? No! Murder is a legal definition of an unlawful killing. I do not advocate murder! But if you kill someone, you *will* answer in a court of law (more on this in Chapter Nine). You may win or lose depending on the circumstances, but at least you will have the chance to be heard. If you flunk your "life" test, you will never have the chance.

You may note that earlier I used the word "destroy" rather than "stop." I believe the difference in the two actions is the difference between surviving the encounter or not. In any attempt to stop a violent action, the implied thought is that you will limit your response to just that amount of force necessary to make the problem go away. This is, in general, the law of self-defense. What is the penalty for miscalculating the amount of "stop?" With "destroy," there's no possibility of under-estimation. I'm saying you should use sufficient force (as provided for by law) to "stop" the attack, but I'm also telling you it's better to over-estimate the amount of "stop" necessary, rather than come up short and lose your life or the life of a family member.

Example: You're out hunting and about to face a grizzly bear. Intellectually, you know that a 30-06 cartridge is sufficient, but you have the option of using a .458 Winchester Magnum round. You shoot both rounds equally well. Which cartridge do you choose? There's no contest; you pick the .458. Well, the same thing holds true when dealing with two-legged predators. As African hunter and writer Robert Ruark said, "use enough gun!"

Confronting your adversary is no less dangerous than taking on a grizzly!

The argument is often made that "all he wants is... (fill in the blanks). So don't resist, give him what he demands." OK, this does work, but not always. You should be prepared for the problem to escalate. What happens if he isn't satisfied with what you give him? The "just give it to him" people don't address that issue. And they conveniently ignore many examples of what has been done to victims after they "just gave it to him."

Quoting again from the *Philadelphia Inquirer* article, a 17-year-old who shot an assistant county prosecutor in the back of the head while the man was at an Automated Teller Machine said, "For real, he brung this on himself."

The young killer said that his victim had failed to follow a basic rule of robberies. When approached by a thief, do what he says. "Give it up," the teenager said. "If he'd have done that, the man would still be here. If you hesitate, somebody gonna give it to you. Shoot you," he said.

Of course, surrendering quickly assumes that you have a crystal ball that will assure you that Otherhuman will not hurt you or your family if you comply immediately with his every demand. Oh, sure! This social crap of quiet compliance didn't work in Nazi Germany and it won't work anywhere else now. (Just recently in Philadelphia, a well-liked and respected pharmacist in a nice, middle-class neighborhood was killed, even though he gave the perpetrators the drugs they were seeking. And I know this is happening in other neighborhoods around the country; just read your local newspapers.)

There are a few problems with immediate and total resistance to a predatory confrontation, of course. The primary problem is recognizing that you are involved in one soon enough to take any action. For instance, here are some descriptions of real-life muggings.

The victim drives a school bus. He has a concealed weapons permit, practices regularly with his handgun and carries it with him all the time except when driving the bus, since he's prohibited by his employer from doing so.

One nice sunny day, he drives the kiddies to the big city on a day-trip to a museum. Kiddies are off and he takes a walk to see the sights. He's walking, in broad daylight, on a wide sidewalk in the center city area. He notices three young males walking toward him in a group. They split, one to the right and two to the left, as they approach him. The guy on the right side hits the bus driver in the stomach as he walks by. The three then take his wallet and watch as he writhes in pain on the pavement. The mugging, for that's what it was, was over in the proverbial blink of an eye. The three men grabbed the loot and continued their leisurely walk away from the victim.

Another mugging. Two middle-aged males pull their van into the parking lot of a convenience store at lunch time. As they park, two large males, disheveled and wearing work clothes, shove their faces into the driver's open window and yell that their car is broken down and they need $7.87 to fix a fan belt. They didn't ask for help, they asked for money and glared at the driver and his passenger. They got $5 from the driver, who appeared too stunned to do anything else.

This was indeed a mugging, albeit mugging by extortion, intimidation and fear. Subsequent investigation showed that both men had been in the area for hours working the same "mugging" technique.

How does the reality of these muggings square with the experts' advice? The admonition to "give it up" usually does work if done quickly and without hesitation. Eye contact should also be avoided, since you don't want to do anything to piss him off. (Quoting from the *Inquirer* article again, a 16-year-old and two friends were walking through a public park one October day when they came upon a university student on his way home from a touch football game. The 16-year-old picked up a tree limb, smashing the student's skull and, as he lay dying, took $11.61 from his pockets. The 16-year-old later told authorities that he felt obligated to kill him because the student had looked him in the eye!)

The cold hard fact is that there is no single, identifiable attribute or "type" of Otherhumans. They don't carry signs or wear particular clothing that will let you readily identify them. (Excluding the "gang-banger" kind, of course.) They're not any particular color or nationality and you will surely flunk "living" if you only become wary around certain classes of citizens or in certain neighborhoods. For instance, the informant I mentioned earlier in this Chapter was a pleasantly-fat, middle-aged man who looked a bit like Uncle Remus from the old "Br'er Rabbit" tale — except for his eyes. Otherhuman is identified only by his actions and that leaves you precious little time to stay alive and safe.

If you can understand this concept, you might survive. Otherhuman gives no quarter and you should not tender any to him. Any potentially-lethal encounter is not the time for moral reflection on your actions. You must act immediately, before he can destroy you. Remorse and absolution come later, in the comfort of your family and/or your church.

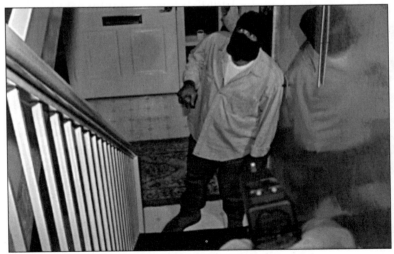

When Otherhuman invades your home, drastic measures are called for!

CHAPTER 3

AWARENESS

Certainly you can win any fight by avoiding it just as well as battling to come out on top — and with a lot less hassle. This is the best way to survive. But there is *avoiding* and there is living in fear. If, as I've described in the previous chapter, Otherhuman is not easily recognizable, strikes without warning and the attack is over in the proverbial blink of an eye, how on earth can anyone avoid such a bolt of lightning?

Simplistically put, one way is — don't be where the lightning strikes. In other words, don't be a lightning rod. If you look and act like a victim, you'll in all probability get to be a victim. Moving rapidly through an environment with your head down and shoulders hunched forward certainly tells the world that you're frightened of something. Moving purposefully, with your head up, shoulders back, looking from side to side, alert to the environment, tells the world that you are not likely to be an easy victim. At a minimum, your "body language" telegraphs to Otherhuman what he can expect if he approaches you. This is not to say that you walk around like General George Patton reviewing the troops. But alert attentiveness will deter some attacks and you'll certainly be ready for the rest.

Ordinary civilians are frequently puzzled and bemused by one cop quickly identifying another cop purely by his atti-

This man's posture or "body language" screams victim to the predator!

Two other men in the same setting. See how different they look?
These two men are not going to be easy targets!

tude. Again, it's a matter of body language. The cop tends to stand and walk as if he owns the very earth that he happens to be occupying at the time. It's territorial. This posture is necessary if the cop is to be effective, but cops carry this attitude over into off-duty hours and might as well carry a sign reading "cop." In fact, decoy cops have to work to break themselves of this "I own the earth" posture, otherwise they're not very good at decoy work. Curiously, they learn to act like civilians to encourage an assault. (Could it be there's something to be learned from this?)

It can be argued that it's all well and good for the cops to act this way. After all, they're armed with a badge and a gun, but civilians are pretty much naked of lawful authority. How does one act with authority if he doesn't have any? Well, you need to have some inner pride, confidence in your own abilities to survive and, as I've said before, learn to manage your fears. Again, I'm not advocating false courage. There are some situations where the best thing to do is run or give up your money. There's not much satisfaction in being "dead" right!

Even while at rest, be wary. This man is relaxing in the sun in front of his warehouse, but he's still alert to any sign of trouble.

In essence, I'm saying, "Walk like a free man." Be aware of your environment, all the time, day or night, awake or asleep. We didn't drop to earth in our present form. We have been taught that we evolved over thousands of years from a very simplistic hunter-gatherer society to our present "modern" civilized state of being. Don't accept this premise. We're *still* hunter-gatherers. We just do it differently now than when we first started. We also still have all those abilities that enabled us to survive back then. We just don't acknowledge — or we block out — their existence. We have become so civilized that we're brain dead — at least the part of the brain that tells us when we're threatened on a personal and deadly level.

As you bounce through life, you do see the threats and dangerous positions. You just don't let yourself accept what your brain is telling you. For instance, in most large cities you can see a mugging coming if you know the signs. It will probably go something like this. You're walking down a street. Two men are walking up the street toward you. You're 15 yards from each other on a collision course. You step to the left to pass them.

Normally, the two men would step to *their* left at the same time. But this time, it appears you've all got your signals mixed. When you step left they step *right*, directly into your new path. No problem, just mixed signals. So you step back to your right to effect passage. Only they both step left, along with you, so now they're still in your path as the distance between you rapidly closes. Guess what? You're about to be mugged. And that's the only "signal" you're going to get, so you need to learn to pick up on such signs quickly. Back on the street, you now either rapidly cross to the other side, if you can, or brace yourself to deal with the problem head on. The thoroughly-civilized, "brain-dead" man sees this same pattern, but immediately dismisses it — and is mugged!

In American society, there's a certain amount of space that is maintained between people when they talk to one another during a meeting or when they pass by each other on the street. If someone gets inside your "space," he is a potential threat. Don't evaluate the age, sex, race or size of the person; just maintain your space or increase your defensive awareness. If you try to evaluate and judge each possible threat, you soon tire of it and you are right back to being a victim.

One personal example: My friend and I had stopped at an isolated, small-town gas station about 5:00 PM. A white cargo van was on the other side of the pump. The driver got out of the van to get gas. He was a white male in his 40s, wearing work clothes. He glanced at us and our car repeatedly. Another, older man, a white male in his 70's, medium build, dressed in casual clothes, appeared and began talking to the first man.

As they talked, the older man kept shifting his position closer and closer to us. Finally he had, as far as I was concerned, moved into my "space" and I prepared for an encounter. I didn't "evaluate" the adversary. (He's either too close or he's not.) I shifted my body stance and engaged him in conversation. Nothing happened. But if you think that considering a 70-year-old man a threat is over-reacting, did you forget about the van driver in his 40s?

Jeff Cooper has tried to teach awareness via a color code to show you various states of awareness and preparations to fight or flee. Giving someone a color or numerical code to follow helps, but you need to understand what you're looking at or experiencing. A better answer is both simple and complex. You must *know your enemy*, as we discussed in Chapter Two, and you must also strive to be totally *aware* at all times.

Here's a little experiment that will help you learn how to let your mind be "aware." Find yourself a comfortable chair, a quiet place with no visual distractions. Relax. Feel the chair against your body. Feel the floor beneath

To thwart a potential carjacking, drive through them to get away if you can. However, you should be aware enough to see it coming! (This driver didn't, and now he has a big problem; he can't just pull forward and drive away.)

your feet. As you sit still, feel the circulation of air against you. As you "feel" these things, start to listen. Modern man spends most of his time tuning out distractions so that he can focus on the problems at hand. I'm suggesting that you relearn that which you experienced as a baby. Learn to experience your entire environment. You can be aware of the earth beneath your feet, the wind, the sounds of your world. A simplistic exercise? I don't believe so. As you re-learn to let your mind sense the world around you, your brain will start getting acclimated to continual testing of your immediate area.

As your senses redevelop, you will begin to be able to notice if there's someone nearby without seeing him. This, then, is awareness. As you expand your abilities, you will also "pick up" on others' aggressive intentions.

Of course, Otherhuman "reads" you, as well. You give off non-verbal, conscious and unconscious "emanations," for lack of a better word, and he reads them instantly. Fear can be smelled. You can taste your own fear — brassy, most likely. Strong emotions such as anger and hatred can strike you or your opponent like a physical blow. Note this well: you **can** learn to read all these emotions. You can also learn to mask all your own emotions so that they are not easily read by an opponent.

You might think that you would always want the bad guy to know your state of mind so that the problem could be avoided. In general, this is true and can be practiced on a regular basis. But sometimes you may well be the aggressor on the good guys' side and you don't want to alert your quarry as you prepare to strike.

Stalking is an art in itself. The predator will pick up on your intentions if you make no effort to conceal them and he'll be gone. Try a simple experiment. Stare intently at someone at some distance. Watch how he reacts to your focus. He'll eventually seek you out, if he doesn't leave the area first. You've probably done this exercise already; most men have. Look too long at an attractive woman and she'll turn and notice you, oft times to your embarrassment.

All of this works conversely, as well. If you "feel" you're being observed, you probably are. Modern man has spent several lifetimes trying to be "civilized," with the net result that we have learned to ignore what our cave-men ancestors knew instinctively. I've found that those persons who work with the land and with animals are more able to read these signals than are those who are shut up in cities. There is such a thing as being *too* civilized.

Jeff Cooper's color code to denote degrees of awareness is well known thanks to his numerous writings and training courses. White is described as being asleep or completely unaware of what is going on around you. Yellow is the condition of wariness wherein you do take note of your world. Orange is a heightened state of yellow, where you key onto a specific threat and begin to develop a plan of action. Red is when you are waiting for the threat to occur. You realize that a lethal response will probably be necessary and you're in total readiness. Clint Smith of Thunder Ranch has added the color black, to denote that the fight is on, the battle rages, the clash has occurred.

Cooper rightly claims that you can live your life in condition yellow — cautious of your world, taking note of everyone and everything. Critics have described this way of life as being "paranoid," suggesting that you're looking for a goblin under every bush. Not at all. A better description of condition yellow is that you simply take a fresh and skeptical look at everything *every time you look at it.* Most of us come home everyday to the same house in the same neighborhood. Normally, we make the assumption that everything is the "same" as it has always been, so we don't really take a good look at our sur- roundings *at that moment.* Well, if you continue this assumption of sameness for the rest of everyday living — and most people do — it can be fatal. It is said that if you have not met with a man for three days, look at him closely, for he has changed.

I suggest that you look at and observe everything not unlike an innocent baby; in other words, with no prior assumptions. You then are much more observant and can see a threat where you previously "assumed" all was safe.

The next notch up is living in condition red. Now, there are those who can and do live in this condition all the time. Front-line soldiers are the best example of living in this mental state. They are always primed and ready to react violently to any perceived threat. This has been described as having no future, no past, no friends...just living in the moment of time, poised to strike.

According to some, this state of being can't be maintained for long periods of time. This both is, and is not, correct. It can be lived in for years. It is also truly a very corrosive way of life. The individual in this always-ready-to-go state of mind is a very dangerous threat to anyone who might trespass into his territory. It's a mindset that is good for war, but very little else. Be this as it may, I've lived this way and personally know of others who have also done so. None of us want to repeat the experience, however.

As debilitating as living in condition red is to one's mental health, some of its attributes can be adapted to a more realistic mindset. If you work or travel constantly in a very hostile environment, you can pre-program yourself to eliminate one step in the self-defense process. Normally there is stimuli, thought and response. You see the threat, decide what action to take and then complete the action. If you skip the thought process, you radically increase your survival quotient.

Usually, for example, if someone jabs you in the back, you're startled. Then you think, "Why has someone or something done this?" You look to see what and who is causing the action and then decide what to do about it. This takes too long. In a hostile or high-risk area, if you're poked in the back, react. Turn, block or otherwise move from the possible threat. In short, *stimuli must equal response.* This needs to be tempered, of course, for you don't get invited back to too many parties if you react this way at the punch bowl!

If this mindset is practiced enough to become second nature, your chances of always coming out on top increase dramatically. Of course, you also run the risk of wrongful, mistaken actions and early death due to system-overload on your body. The trick is to find the correct balance for the life you live. That's a very personal decision which should not be dictated to you by others. Choose carefully, for you will live or die based on the results.

Author shows how homeowner can be unobtrusively armed when unexpected visitors arrive. (Note the handgun hidden underneath the newspaper in second photo.)

CHAPTER 4

WEAPONS IN THE BAD GUY'S ARSENAL

It's all well and good to have the right gun, holster, ammo, training and be in the proper state of mind to defend yourself, but it helps a lot if you know who and what you're going up against. I've explained how Otherhuman views you and the world, but we haven't talked about the tools he uses.

In the real world, the object of an attack is to succeed by and with whatever means possible. Otherhuman isn't hung up on "which is the right gun for you?" or "is the 9mm better than the .45ACP?". Yes, handguns, sawed-off shotguns and rifles are in the bad guy's repertoire of tools, but not always or even as often as the government and media scare-mongers would have you believe. A good handgun, for instance, is cash-in-hand in its own right and may well be sold to get Otherhuman's current drug of choice.

Understand that Otherhuman is the sort of person who will literally break into a neighboring apartment or house just to steal food off the kitchen table, simply because he's hungry and the food is there. Otherhuman uses whatever tool is available to achieve his goal, be it a gun, knife, brick, board, tree limb or any other item that will serve as a weapon.

The government may have managed to prohibit or severe-ly restrict the flow of conventional guns to particular areas, but that is small solace when you encounter those who have learned to improvise to fill their needs. Consider this: in maximum security prisons, periodic shakedowns *always* produce some sort of homemade weapons. If the prisoners can get or make weapons and kill or abuse each other, how can you believe that Otherhuman hasn't figured out how to arm himself well enough to get whatever he wants?

For example, in the major metropolitan area with which I'm most familiar — the city and environs of Philadelphia, PA — it's not uncommon to see men, particularly older men, walking with a "cane." I emphasize the word "cane" because they aren't using what we think of when we read the word "cane," — usually a straight shaft, about 39 inches long, with a curved hook or handle at the top end and a rubber crutch tip on the other (although this is a very good defensive tool in its own right). These men don't use the normal cane; they improvise with a "cane" that is about one to three inches thick and often still has the tree limb stubs on it. In reality, the older men, and some of the younger ones as well, are carrying clubs. In the case of the older men, the canes are defensive tools against men and dogs, but such a tool is neutral in that it can be offensive or defensive, depending on the user. These "canes" have much more resemblance to a poor man's Irish shillelagh.

In fact, homemade weapons are much more common than guns. For instance, the "cane" I just described, a broken car antenna, a piece of steel sharpened and wrapped with tape (the classic prison "shank") or a piece of glass wrapped with a rag. Even an ordinary brick, rock or broken piece of concrete, for that matter. If you stop

and think about some of these tools, they're ideal. Otherhuman uses them and loses them. That way, there are no weapons to be found at the scene and none to be carried away and found on any suspect. Who would bother to search through a pile of rubble in a vacant lot to identify a particular piece of rock used to bash someone's head in?

This savvy gentleman not only carries a defensive "stick" when he goes out for his morning newspaper, he takes his dog along, as well.

You need to watch for and really "see" what the other guy's got in his hands. You may well read his intent correctly but dismiss your observation because you don't see any recognizable weapon. Just because someone is carrying a shopping bag doesn't mean he's going to the grocery store. You might be the store and the bag may have a brick in it!

Old barroom fighters already know this one, but you should realize that a full bottle of beer, preferably capped, is a very good blunt object. (For non-drinkers, a glass ketchup bottle is just as good.) As you walk by a group of corner loungers drinking their "40s" (40-ounce bottles of malt liquor) wrapped in paper bags, be aware that you're going past a group of armed and possibly drunk men with weapons already in hand.

Other neat tricks I've seen: the "roofer" or "carpenter" going about his business on the street. He's got his hammer, cardboard box cutter or folding knife on his belt, in his back pocket or in a carpenter's apron. The police have no reason to detain him, yet he's well armed and his draw is a damn sight faster than yours.

Another unconventional weapon and often the weapon of choice, especially in Philadelphia — the ubiquitous baseball bat (and hockey sticks to a lesser degree). Who would question one or two men walking down the street with baseball bats and gloves? Of course, you may be the ball! By the way, if I've been in one house in the city that had a bat or an axe handle just inside the front door, I've been in a thousand. And bats, axe handles, pick handles, hockey sticks, broomsticks, shovels and even golf clubs are great fighting tools.

More food for thought. If you saw a man wearing greasy mechanic's coveralls with a little name tag on his chest, you might not pay much attention to the ten-inch screwdriver in his back pocket — until he stabs you with it. In reality, what can be used as a killing or maiming device is only limited by the individual's inventiveness and imagination. These techniques work both ways, of course. The good guy, too, can use any or all of them where he is precluded from using more-conventional arms.

Another, more formal, weapon of choice for the good guys locally is what is known as the "Philadelphia deer rifle." This is a pump-action shotgun hanging on a wall gun rack in an upstairs bedroom or is stashed in the trunk or on the back seat of a car. The only thing is, it's loaded with slugs or buckshot and ready to go as it's hanging there among the stuffed squirrel and ringneck pheasant trophies or carefully placed on top of a hunting jacket, complete with current hunting license. Twenty-two caliber rifles are also popular because they make almost no noise. (In some areas, the normal neighborhood sounds are enough to effectively "silence" a .22 rifle.) They're easy to shoot well and easy to justify having when stopped or questioned by the authorities.

Take this instance of using a .22 rifle effectively. Two cars were going up a one-way, two-lane-wide city street. The car in the front wasn't going fast enough to suit the trailing driver, who decided to "bump" the lead car to get him to move a bit faster. It worked. The lead car sped up enough to gain a few blocks' advantage. The driver then stopped, got out, opened his trunk, removed his fully-loaded semi-auto tubular-fed .22 rifle and waited for the "bumper" to arrive. When the second car got close, the man emptied the .22 at the impatient driver, then turned back, threw the .22 in the trunk, closed it and drove leisurely away. The act was witnessed, but no one was ever identified in the matter.

So far, the gender orientation we've been discussing has been male. But we all know the female of the species is the deadlier. Any woman has the right to carry a comb stuck in her hair. She (and of course he) can also use the "pick" end to good advantage. (Some magazine ads offer "Ice Pick" knife/hair combs for sale that have a stiletto in the handle.) Would you think twice about walking past someone who was just fussing with his or her hair? And what about the women who carry single-edge razor blades? (Yes, some of them do, so be prepared.)

Earlier, I mentioned knives. Everyone's got one and knives don't run out of ammo or jam. If the user has half a brain (which he usually does), he can always stop at one of the cheaper steak restaurants and pick up a very good knife. (It has to be very good — to cut the tough steak they sell.) Women particularly like knives and those single-edge razor blades we mentioned. There you are, busy checking them out and they check you out — of your money, if not your life. Along with the obvious distraction of an attractive woman, most men don't consider women a threat to start with and then are very reluctant to hit them if need be, let alone consider using deadly force. Park your chivalry and ego, guys. Men, women and children can and do kill!

In some states, the sale of pepper spray is prohibited to civilians. Big deal. Instead, Otherhuman might just throw lye in your face. In addition to bats behind the door, many people (at least in large cities) will keep a can of lye near the front door or along side their bed in addition to the ubiquitous large kitchen knife. (Human urine is often added to the lye, by the way. Why? Just because it makes the potion more vile. Urine adds nothing to the effectiveness of the lye, but stop and think about the mindset of someone who does this.) On the whole, I would rather have everyone be allowed to buy and use pepper spray.

The point of this chapter on unconventional weapons is to show that you can't assume *anything* about your adversary. If you're uneasy about a person or situation, listen to what I call "the little man in the back of my head." He tells me when things aren't right and I listen — and live.

One last thought. There's always a great deal of idiotic chatter about cheap handguns...that they're ineffective, inaccurate, unreliable. (Of course, this usually comes from those with plenty of money. Nobody ever asks what poor people think.) Well, I can attest to three things.

Cheap handguns kill. Cheap handguns are accurate. Cheap handguns are reliable.

I asked Bob Thomsen, a friend of mine who's a police officer and a very good shot, to take a Lorcin .380ACP semi-auto that I had on hand for Test and Evaluation to the range and see just what he could expect to get out of the gun shooting it at a measured 37 yards. Why 37 yards? Well, not coincidentally, the local media had carried an account of a woman who had been sitting on her front step on Mischief Night (the night before Halloween) chatting away on the cordless phone in her hand. A group of neighborhood "teenagers" saw her and thought it would really be amusing to pelt her with raw eggs.

After the egg attack, she went back into her house, armed herself with a Lorcin .380 semi-auto loaded with Federal Hydra-Shok ammo and came back outside to sit on her front step, still talking on her cordless phone. The "teenagers," having run out of "ammunition," went to a nearby store and got a few dozen more eggs. They then went back to pelt the woman again. Bad move. As the one 6-foot-plus, 200-pound, 18-year-old teenager advanced on her throwing eggs, she "threw" one round of .380 ammo at him at a measured 37 yards. She later claimed that she only wanted to frighten him off. It was not his night, for her "scare" round entered his temple and exited the back of his head, killing him instantly.

Thomsen fired the sample Lorcin from a braced, kneeling position at a B-27 police target. The seven-shot group of Remington UMC FMJ ammo placed four inches low and to the left of point-of-aim and measured six inches across. I've had this .380 Lorcin for a year and it has never jammed or failed to operate with factory ball ammo. (A corresponding gun chambered for the .22LR round might as well have been a boat anchor, though, for it rarely fired more than one or two rounds before jamming. But then again, who wants to be shot with "only" one or two rounds of .22LR ammo?)

The bottom line? In a confrontation, don't get snobbish or hung up on tools. And remember, anything that Otherhuman can use against you, you can use against him to defend yourself. A shovel in hand beats a gun in the drawer every time!

These are just some of the weapons actually used or carried by the predators out there. (They were confiscated by a suburban township police department in Southeastern Pennsylvania.)

CHAPTER 5

CHOOSING YOUR WEAPON

Once you've decided to make a commitment to develop the proper mindset, sense of awareness and knowledge of the enemy that is needed for you to be able to defend yourself and your family adequately, you must choose a weapon. You must look into yourself and decide with what type of defensive tool you are most comfortable. A firearm is not the answer for everyone. Based on religious or philosophical beliefs, some folks cannot and will not use deadly force against another human being, regardless of the provocation. In this chapter as well as Chapter 12, you'll find suggestions for alternative tools that injure or incapacitate and are only capable of deadly force if used to the extreme. Tear gas or pepper sprays are examples of self-defense means that may give you time to remove yourself from the immediate threat. Naturally, the first criteria in selecting a weapon for personal defense is complete familiarity with the prevailing laws in your state.

If you are restricted from having a gun or can own only certain types of guns, your choices become limited very quickly. If firearms ownership is not permitted at all, then you must fall back to choosing from knives and clubs, tools which can be used with lethal results if absolutely necessary. Less-than-lethal tools, such as tear gas and pepper sprays, are certainly defense options but, in my opinion and experience, they rank as a poor second choice.

If you choose any of the pepper sprays, spray and run!

The sprays are somewhat effective, of course, and are used most appropriately by police who must control the amount of force used during an arrest. However, for a private citizen who is faced with deadly force — rape, kidnapping or other any other life-threatening act — using a less-than-lethal-force option is foolhardy. Brave, but foolhardy. I won't belabor the matter other than to say there are so many conditions upon which the spray's use depends as to make this choice a charade for the user. A knife or club is a much better weapon.

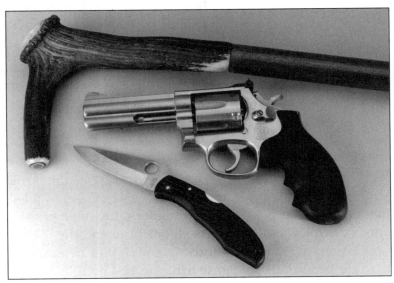

These weapons run the gamut from primitive to sophisticated, but all are useful for self-defense.

I know that if I'm armed with a baseball bat and I hit a "home run," I can reasonably expect certain results. If I miss on my home run and only get a single, I can repeat my batting practice immediately, with more attention and enthusiasm. If I pepper spray an attacker, I don't know if the spray has worked, since there's a reaction time of from one to three seconds. By then, it's too late for any action other than a re-application of the spray, which at that point is useless, as the attacker is upon me.

In addition to which, in some locales pepper spray and tear gas are not legal for use by non-law enforcement individuals. No big deal. You *can* carry hair spray or oven cleaner. Hair spray is an eye irritant and most oven cleaner has lye in it. As we pointed out in the previous chapter, in the poorer sections of large cities, the inhabitants have long kept a pan or jar of lye handy at the door or at their bedside. (Note of caution to new police officers, in case no one ever pointed this out: *don't trust a man or woman who answers the door holding what appears to be an innocuous dish, glass or pan!)*

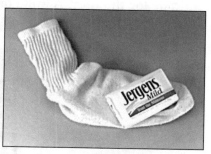

A bar of soap in a sock; an improvised self-defense tool.

If your weapon of choice for personal defense is a firearm, you must reckon with the potential consequences of taking a life. Yes, in many, many instances, the mere presence or display of a firearm is sufficient to end the assault, but not with absolute certainty. After determining that you are permitted to arm yourself both by law and by your beliefs, you now need to decide upon the firearm. In almost all cases, it will be a handgun. Now, this is not to say that a handgun is the ideal defensive arm; it's chosen to deal with the unanticipated attack. But where concealed carry is permitted, you can have it with you all the time, and it will neither alert the predator nor disturb others with whom you come in contact.

Finding a gun with which you are comfortable and can work effectively has been the stuff of thousands of articles and a great many books. The titles are all a variation of "which is the right gun for you?," with the author telling you, who he doesn't know, what gun you should use for self-defense or carry in your daily life pursuits. How egotistical, presumptuous and stupid.

Big or little, all handguns are effective within their individual limitations.

Are you short, tall, fat, thin, young, old, enfeebled, lame, athletic or sedentary? Do you work in a business suit or casual clothes? Are you a professional in daily contact with other professionals in an urban setting? Where do you live? Have you been threatened or menaced? None of this is known and, more pointedly, none of these conditions are addressed in the usual article that touts revolver or semi-auto brand A, caliber type B and holster brand C.

Following are just a few examples of the variables in gun selection.

Example one: A professional businessman calls on clients in a large metropolitan city. He wants to be armed, but also knows that if this fact became known to his clients, he'd be considered a "nut case" and many of them would never do business with him again. One lawyer I know carries a Seecamp .32ACP. He's always armed, but never offends.

Example two: A shopkeeper, just starting out on the economic ladder, runs a convenience store in the poorer section of one of the largest US cities. He has taken a job that others have moved away from. He knows the dangers, but the rent's cheap and there's a viable market for his services. If he's known not to be armed, he'll be out of business and possibly out of life in short order. But if he's seen to be armed during his daily business, he'll offend most of the decent citizens who are his customers. One owner of a check cashing agency has solved this dilemma. He carries a Charter Arms .38 Special 2"-barreled revolver in a cheap clip-on inside-the-pants holster worn in the small of his back. (He's also surrounded by bullet-resistant glass.)

Example three: A middle-class homeowner living in a middle-class neighborhood with a couple of teenage kids who are the product of modern schooling. The home resembles a train station, with all the comings and goings of the kids and their friends. He keeps his custom Colt

10mm Delta Elite on a closet shelf and a loaded magazine in his pocket. He runs a cash business and brings the cash home with him at night. At work, he carries a Beretta .25 semi-auto in his front pants pocket, keeps a 6" Colt .357 caliber revolver in his truck and a 12-gauge Remington 18"-barrel pump shotgun and two Rottweiler dogs in his warehouse.

Example four: A retired couple, in their late 60s or early 70s, traveling the USA in their RV. What does our polyester pair use for defense? One old soldier and RV traveler I know, a former Olympic shooter, has a Colt AR-15 Sporter in .223 caliber stashed in a closet with the magazine loaded but out of the gun.

You get the point. Which gun, if any, answers their individual needs? Just what gun should they have and what can they legally get or financially afford? Obviously, there's no pat answer to the four problems presented and I can go on for pages with additional problems that will also not lend themselves to pat solutions.

The answer to all the scenarios is to make a selection based on need, economics, training and, of course, the prevailing state laws concerning firearms. In fairness to the authors of "right gun" articles, they do present the best features of their particular choices so that the reader might make an informed decision.

If you put the listed criteria in a matrix, you can see that the shopkeeper got an inexpensive handgun. The old warrior in the RV keeps a rifle close at hand. The mobile urban professional went for a high-end mini-handgun, while the middle-class suburbanite chose a range of guns to fit his various locales.

When choosing a firearm, most any modern gun will suffice for personal protection in your home, car, work place or on your person. If your local laws only permit shotguns, your shotgun choices begin with a single-barrel, break-open type with exposed hammer, progress through the double-barrel, with or without exposed hammers, move to the slide-action or pump shotgun and end with the semi-auto guns.

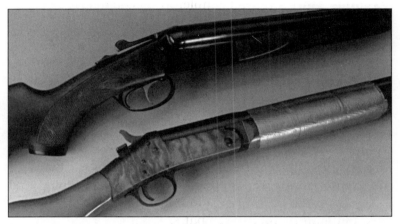

The single-barrel, break-open-type shotgun (bottom) is the simplest to operate. The double-barreled shotgun (top) is more complicated, but gives you two shots.

This progression also mirrors the cost and complexity of operation. The single-barrel shotgun, with exposed hammer that must be cocked after the chamber is loaded, is virtually idiot-proof and can be learned in a few minutes by anyone who has at least an IQ at or above room temperature. The double-barrel, side-by-side shotgun requires more attention to mechanical safety but gives the user two shots on demand. The double has one other big plus. Almost everyone on the planet will recognize the double-barrelled shotgun as a *shotgun*. There's no mistaking the two gaping barrels pointed at you for a big pipe or a broomstick. For the little value of intimidation that any weapon possesses, the side-by-side ranks at the top of the list.

During my law enforcement career, the pump-action shotgun was standard issue. Since retiring from the job, I've found that I choose the side-by-side more often, because I want the bad guy to instantly realize he's looking at a 12-gauge, not a metal pipe. I'm looking for deterrence rather than volume of fire. I accept the fact that deterrence might not work and I'll be left with only a two-shot arm, but that's my choice.

These pump-action shotguns in either configuration (fixed stock, top; folding stock with pistol grip, bottom) are good choices to keep in your home or recreational vehicle.

However, if you do choose a pump-action shotgun for defense, you must realize that there's a longer learning curve to operating the arm — loading and unloading — as well as learning to *reflexively* release the safety. On balance, though, the short-barreled pump-action shotgun is a wondrous tool because you can more easily aim it than a handgun. (You have four points of support for the shotgun: both hands, your shoulder and your cheek. With a handgun, you only have your hands and arms.) Most pump shotguns hold from five to eight rounds of pellet or slug ammunition and either is very effective at close range. Of course, a pump-action shotgun is less effective than a good club if you don't spend the necessary time learning to master its intricacies.

The author's wife, Katherine, shooting a Benelli 12-gauge semi-auto shotgun, shows her determination to master the semi-automatic shotgun for home defense.

The semi-automatic shotgun, where a round is fired each time the trigger is pulled, is an excellent defense arm if you learn to manipulate it correctly. It is more intricate to load and unload than the pump-action or the break-open action shotguns. Any of the shotguns, with solid shot (slugs) rather than multiple projectile loads (buckshot), in the hands of a well-trained man can be effective to a distance of 50 yards and even to 100 yards with extensive practice. By and large though, this is the exception rather than the rule and the shotgun is at its best up close, used against a threat no farther away than 25 yards.

The rifle is, unarguably, the premier defense arm. It has both offensive and defensive capability and certainly has enough "punch" when chambered for any center-fire cartridge. Remember, too, that most rifle rounds will defeat ordinary body armor. It's something to keep in mind, because the bad guys often wear body armor and use rifles, so this "advantage" can work against you.

Some of the negatives of using a rifle are a reverse listing of its attributes. As I pointed out, it has more than enough "punch" to do the job. This translates into the reality of the rifle bullet being the most penetrative of all commonly-owned small arms. The rifle's renowned accuracy is due in no small part to its being fired, as is the shotgun, with two hands from the shooter's shoulder, supported by his cheek. This, of course, makes many rifles too long and cumbersome for applications that require concealment. A collapsible stock is a good option, but must be extended for effective rifle accuracy.

Whatever the caliber or action type, a rifle delivers more accurate shots at a farther distance than any handgun or shotgun. (Rifles, top to bottom: bolt-action, semi-auto and single-shot.)

The author, shooting an M-16 rifle during his Drug Enforcement Administration (DEA) Submachine Gun Instructor qualification training at the FBI Academy range in Quantico, VA.

However, given these negatives, the isolated homeowner, the occasional hunter, the recreational high-power rifle shooter all have an arm that will do double duty. Sure, a single-shot .22 rimfire target rifle, complete with hooked buttplate and affixed palm rest, is cumbersome to handle, but it certainly will deliver its one round with pinpoint accuracy. And single-shot rifles are really not all that slow to reload, either.

In one instance, a female attorney I know had received a nice Browning over and under 12-gauge trap shotgun and a single-shot .22LR Winchester match rifle in lieu of attorney fees. She approached me to sell the shotgun. I asked her what she intended to do with the .22, and she said she was keeping it for home protection. I pointed out that the shotgun was better for the job, but she knew that the shotgun would bring more in a sale and she needed the money. She realized the limitations of the .22, but added that she had small children and the .22 could be made safe easily while she retained control of the ammo. (Good choice or not, she had thought the matter through and did have a plan.)

And there's a sequel to this example. The lawyer was burglarized and the single-shot .22 was taken. She's replaced it with a magazine-fed .22 rifle and carries the magazine in her pocket, with the rifle secured in a closet.

If a military surplus rifle is selected, you have the best of two worlds — a battle-tested design that is priced very reasonably. Recently, an observer of the military firearms market commented that the Russian-designed and Comblock-manufactured SKS semi-automatic 10-shot magazine-fed rifle, chambered in 7.62x39 Russian, could well arm every man in the USA. They've been imported by the millions and prices have ranged from $89 to $250, with plenty of cheap surplus ammo to boot.

In fact, all the various rifles available — single-shot, bolt-action, semi-auto, tube-fed, clip-fed, magazine-fed, new, used or surplus — all preferably in some center-fire round, are practical for self-defense.

As far as traveling with firearms, the sporting rifle and sporting shotgun (that old double-barrel) are the least likely to raise the eyebrows of law enforcement authorities, regardless of the locale. If a semi-auto is more to your liking, as it is to mine, the M-1 Garand slides nicely into a non-offensive-looking rifle case and it's damn quick to load with the 8-round en bloc clip. An M-1 carbine also fits this category nicely. With a rifle, a man truly commands all he surveys!

Two time-tested battle rifles — the Russian-designed SKS (top); the M-1 Garand (bottom).

That said, if the law where you reside allows you to own and/or carry a handgun, this certainly gets my vote as the most versatile weapon of the self-defense choices. (Although it has been said, correctly, that you use a handgun to fight your way back to the rifle you should not have put down.)

CHAPTER 6

TYPES OF SELF-DEFENSE HANDGUNS

I f you are considering using a handgun for self-defense rather than a rifle or shotgun, it should be understood that most any modern handgun is more than adequate for personal protection. (This includes the many military surplus handguns, as well.) The man, not the gun, defines and controls the problem.

Having said this, there are a few absolute criteria that any self-defense handgun must meet. Certainly, **the gun must work all the time with the ammo chosen. And it must be able to be fired one-handed, with either hand, while held in any position.** The gun (of course, this is applicable to all defense arms) must not malfunction if fired while turned on its side or upside down. You don't know that you'll always be standing erect when the fight starts or evolves. The gun should not malfunction if held weakly in your hand, either. You might not be in the best of health when trying to use it; you could well have already been attacked and injured.

This is an old, cheap, break-open, throw-away revolver, but it's still capable of defending you — or hurting you.

Any handgun should function reliably, regardless of how it is oriented. If yours won't work in all of these positions, get rid of it!

In addition, **the gun should have plenty of life in it.**
You should be able to practice often, at least once a
month, with a reasonable amount of ammunition, say
fifty rounds or so. (This must be taken into account when
choosing from the military-surplus and used-police-hand-
gun market.)

Naturally, anything man-made will eventually wear out
and firearms are no exception. I strongly recommend taking a page from the Practical Competition Shooters' play
book. They often have three identical handguns: one for
match competition, one as a spare or back-up to the first
and one usually out at the gunsmith being repaired.

Of course, you may not need three guns, but having two
of the same is a good idea. Duplicate your defense gun
and use one for extended practice and one for everyday
carry. You shoot both, but one should be your main practice gun to be heavily used, while the other is shot infre-
quently and reserved for everyday carry. I do this with my
1911s, running one just for competitive use and one for
everyday work. With my S&W Centennial J-frames, I use
the Model 40 steel frame for practice and the aluminum-
frame Model 42 for carry. This puts the most wear on
your "play" gun,
while saving the
duplicate for
defense — and the
"feel" is the same.
There's also no
need to shoot the
most powerful
ammo for practice.
Use standard loads
and only fire the
"buffalo stompers"

A Smith & Wesson Model 42 revolver in a fanny
pack is a "go-anywhere" self-defense setup.

at the end of your practice session. (Practice ammo is less expensive, so you can shoot more.)

Any standard, currently-produced, modern handgun, along with many, but not all, of the military surplus handguns from World War I on, will give faithful service if in good mechanical order and used with the ammunition for which it was designed.

This WWI 1911 was made in 1918, but is still a good semi-auto for self-defense.

For example, a World War I Colt 1911 or Smith & Wesson revolver chambered for .45ACP will not run very long on a diet of modern +P .45 auto ammo, but it will probably last for a good part of your lifetime on GI Hardball or its equivalent. This is not to say either gun will be unsafe with the modern ammo, just that it will break down more quickly with the newest high-velocity stuff. Again, if you have one gun for practice and one for carry, you can avoid early mechanical failure of your primary gun.

This early 20th Century revolver, a WWI 1917 Smith & Wesson, is simple, dependable and affordable.

Getting a *new* gun, like getting a new car, is the best choice. You're not getting someone else's problems this way. But a new gun, like a new car, does need to be used awhile before relying on it. At minimum, you should fire at least 100 rounds of your choice of defensive ammo through the new gun to insure that there are no defects in the product. The gun and ammo combination should work without **any** malfunctions before being considered for defense use.

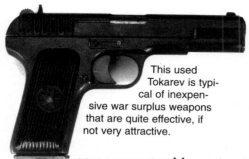

This used Tokarev is typical of inexpensive war surplus weapons that are quite effective, if not very attractive.

Used guns should not necessarily be avoided, however. Not everyone can afford the cost of a new gun, so a used gun is often the only choice. And there are some very good bargains in the used market, particularly among police surplus or trade-ins. Police departments often trade or upgrade for many reasons not related to the efficacy of the particular model. In addition, many of the police trade-ins are refurbished at the factory before being offered for resale. If it worked for them it will work for you, *as long as you don't change anything from the original specs.* Ideally, you should have a qualified gunsmith inspect the gun. (The customizing of guns will be addressed separately in Chapter Eight.)

In choosing a personal defense handgun, there are two main categories: revolvers or semi-automatics. Both have their pluses and minuses. If you choose the revolver, you have a much more simple mechanism with which to become familiar.

Revolvers are more idiot-proof than semi-auto pistols, in that their operation is less complicated. With a double-action revolver, you push or pull on the cylinder release, swing the cylinder out of the frame, insert the cartridges into the chambers, close it and leave it alone. To unload, simply repeat the drill, removing the cartridges by pushing in the extractor rod at the center of the cylinder and the gun is now safe. Quick and neat. Most double-action revolvers require a long, very deliberate ten-pound-plus pull on the trigger to fire the gun in double-action mode, while at the same time offering the option of a more-precise shot by cocking the hammer, which then requires

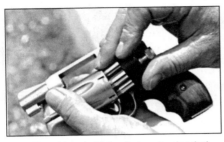
Revolvers are easily loaded and unloaded. A speedloader like the one being used in this photo helps.

only a three- to five-pound, short-movement trigger pull. The revolver is also more "politically correct," having few "bad" media connotations attached to it. (As long as it's not cheaply made, of course.)

The downside of the revolver is that it normally holds only five or six rounds (although there are now some good-quality seven and eight-shot revolvers), as opposed to the semi-autos, which can hold from seven to seventeen rounds. (Although it is highly unlikely that you would need *that many* rounds of ammo to defend yourself.) And revolvers of equal caliber to a semi-auto are more difficult to conceal due to the width of their cylinders and the shape of the hand grip.

Speaking of concealment, this requirement throws the selection process askew. If there is no need for concealment, you can choose the biggest gun with which you are comfortable, revolver or semi-auto. But if you intend to carry it concealed, then its size, weight and shape strongly dictate your selection.

Semi-autos are usually flatter and more compact than any revolvers (with the exception of the North American Arms single-action revolvers, which equal the smallest semi-autos in about equivalent calibers). Thus, the semi-auto is less likely to catch on clothing or dig into your body. The downside is that small semi-autos are picky about ammo and how they're held while firing. In a direct ratio, the smaller the auto the more ammo-sensitive it becomes. When you get to the .25s, you *must* use only full-metal-jacketed round-nose-shaped ammo or else the gun jams. Small, concealable semi-autos have never worked reliably for me in .22 rimfire. If a small semi-auto is your choice, buy the carry one in .25, .32 or .380 caliber and get a like-configured .22 rimfire of the same model, if it's available, for practice. The .22 semi-auto might or might not malfunction, but I wouldn't bet my life on it

Browning .25 (top) and NAA .22 revolver (bottom). Although these calibers are not high on anyone's list of good defense rounds, no one wants to be shot with one!

If you choose a revolver for a concealment gun, some good ones include the Smith & Wesson line of five-shooters of the Model 36 genre, the Colt Detective Special model with its variations of steel or aluminum frames, the Ruger Model 101, the Taurus and the Rossi. They generally weigh from 16 to 32 ounces and are slightly bigger than a man's open hand. Chambered from .22 to .44, compact revolvers offer a wide selection of calibers within the framework of small, easily-concealed handguns.

If you choose a revolver, it should be a double-action design; that is, the first shot is fired by a long pull on the trigger, which not only raises and releases the hammer but also turns and indexes the cylinder, bringing a round in line to be fired.

A single-action revolver, or "cowboy" gun, will work as a defense handgun, but it is not the most efficient action type for the average user to be able to fire multiple shots rapidly. The gun's hammer must be pulled back, or cocked, before the trigger can be pressed to fire each shot. Of course, an argument can be made that this deliberate act of cocking the gun insures against a pre-

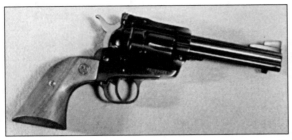

mature discharge, which is true. It is also a slower method of firing a handgun in the hands of all but the most-experienced

The single-action revolvers, although obsolete in design, will deliver five sure shots! Shown is a single-action Ruger .45.

shooter. In addition, you are pointing a "cocked" gun at someone. You will most certainly be viewed as negligent and held criminally and civilly liable in the event of an unintentional firing of the gun.

In semi-automatic handguns, the choice is between the same two action types: single-action or double-action.

The single-action semi-auto requires the firing striker or hammer to be raised, cocked or preloaded against spring tension. The cocked trigger mechanism already has the hammer, or striker, ready to fire. It is only restrained from doing so by some form of mechanically-applied safety, as in the 1911 design, where an external, manually-operated thumb safety must be released. The traditional double-action semi-autos, such as the S&W, Heckler & Koch and Sigarms guns, operate like a double-action revolver for the first shot. They are fired by simply pulling on the trigger without having to remember to move any safety device. The Glock semi-auto falls in between, with its "Safe Action" design (in essence a *short* double action). The Glock has a safety lever that "splits" the trigger down its entire length. The protruding safety has to be depressed in order for the trigger to move back to release the firing striker.

These mechanisms are "safe" in that they will not discharge by themselves; they require one or two deliberate acts to fire. The single-action autos have a large following among Practical Competition shooters because the trigger movement is much shorter and less disturbing to a quickly-aimed shot. However, many people find the thought

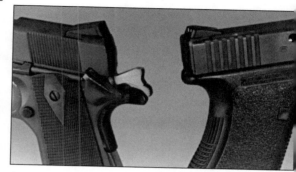

This is a closeup of cocked-and-locked (left) and striker-fired (right) semi-auto handguns.

of carrying a single-action semi-auto 1911 design with the hammer "cocked" and restrained only by mechanical safeties to be abhorrent. For them, the double-action or the Glock Safe-Action semi-autos are the only choices.

There are also some specialty handguns to be considered for defense that don't fall into the revolver or semi-auto categories. For instance, there are small one-, two- and four-shot derringers. These palm-sized pistols are chambered for everything from the .22LR rimfire round up to the .45 Colt cartridge. The mechanism is very simple. It operates the same as the single-action revolver in that the hammer must be pulled back and cocked before being released by the trigger. The barrel(s) are hinged or levered open for loading and unloading. Some of these guns do use a double-action trigger, with a long trigger pull that cocks and releases the firing mechanism. They are effective only at contact distance, for there is no provision for aimed firing, as most guns of this type have no sights. You use them by pointing them at the threat and pulling the trigger. In my experience, I've not found any that were of sufficient quality to hold up to extended

practice firing, with the exception of the discontinued High Standard derringer. (The High Standard derringer was chambered for the .22LR round and had a double-action trigger.) These drawbacks, coupled with the few rounds they hold, put them at the bottom of the list for a defensive handgun.

The demand for small, concealable handguns is timeless. These Sharps derringers from the author's collection date from the mid-1800s.

Fortunately for the U.S. gun user, there's something out there for everyone's tastes, with new models and variations appearing yearly. If you want to be on the "cutting edge" of gun technology, go for it — understand, however, that your experiments may well be real-life "pass or fail" tests. I would advise experimenting with the newest "gadget gun" at the range and going with the tried and true for your personal defense gun.

One last caveat: I've "covered" more than a fair share of suspects with both a revolver and a cocked 1911. I had my finger on the trigger more often than not (a practice not condoned by any instructor!) and I am of the firm opinion that a revolver or double-action semi-auto is much safer to use for the *suspect's* health — and for your subsequent legal defense. It's all too easy to touch off a round from a single-action semi-auto or cocked revolver, no matter how much safe-gun-handling training you've had. And, as I pointed out earlier, you will be viewed as negligent and held criminally and civilly liable in the event of an unintentional firing of the gun.

CHAPTER 7

MASTERING THE GUN

As I pointed out in the previous chapter, a handgun is most often selected for personal defense because of its size and ease of concealment. Caliber is a consideration, but concealability is the first priority. These same attributes work against the ability to easily use it effectively. A long arm, be it a rifle or shotgun, is much easier to hit with than any handgun and a large handgun is easier to shoot than a small one. In all these guns, "bigger" translates into getting skilled more easily.

There is no magical wand that will confer handgun proficiency on the person holding it. Almost no one is born a "natural." Excellent gun skills, particularly with handguns, are only developed after extensive practice. American males seem to think that they're experts on drinking, driving, making love and handgun shooting. But they are dreadfully poor at all these endeavors without instruction and much practice.

Unfortunately, the normal progression of a defensive handgun buyer is to shoot it once or twice at the time of purchase and then the gun is put away, or worse, carried with no further practice — ever. The handgun is loaded and forgotten until it's needed. Realizing that any generalization is fraught with loopholes, I am of the opinion that most self-defense handguns are bought out of fear and placed into use for the same reason. The wonderful mechanism of denial starts to work immediately and the handgun is figuratively and literally pushed to the back of the drawer, usually getting less attention than the person's home smoke detector alarms.

The personal defense gun now has become yet another spare tire in the car of life. The reality is that the tire in the trunk of the car has a much higher probability of accomplishing its goal that does the typical handgun owner with his pistol.

Of course, there are lots of things that we ought to do in life and self-defense training is way down on the list of "things to do this weekend." How to convince yourself or someone else to do otherwise is not easy. Of course, as a reader of this book you are,

The author, practicing at the range with a Glock Model 20 in 10mm.

almost by definition, much more highly motivated to train and practice.

A person who decides to own or carry a firearm for personal defense always has a few basic questions about training or getting proficient with the gun: What kind of training should he get, where should he go to get it and how much will it cost? He knows that he needs to do something and wants to get it over with as soon and as quickly as possible at the lowest cost and with the least amount of inconvenience. Unfortunately, there's almost no "fast food" gun training that's worth much.

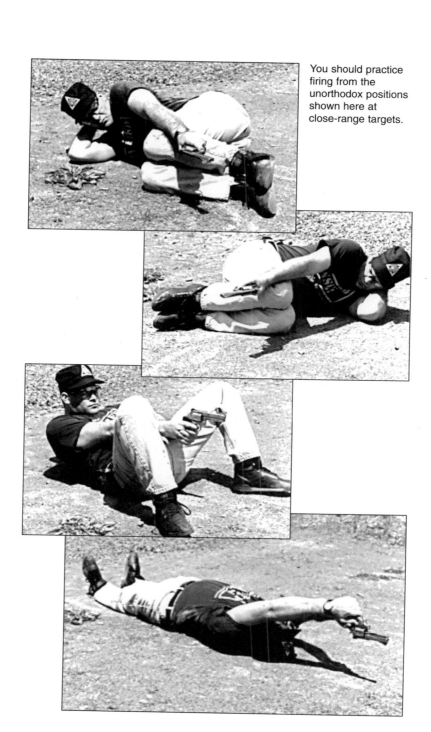

You should practice firing from the unorthodox positions shown here at close-range targets.

If there is no abiding interest in shooting per se, the armed man needs to, at the very least, be able to fire his handgun effectively to a distance of no more than five yards on demand, one-handed or two, from most all normal body positions — standing, sitting, turning and even after being knocked to the ground. Of course, he **must** be able to do this in a life-threatening situation.

Before a student gets into any self-defense training, he must learn to mechanically operate his firearm safely. He must learn the motor skills necessary to deliver a reasonably-accurate shot at no more than five yards. These basic motor skills are best learned in a National Rifle Association Personal Protection Course. Yes, even those of you who have some skill with firearms (see again the American male's concept of proficiency with things). Start (over) at the beginning. At the local volunteer level, the instruction content should be uniformly good. Most local courses will cover gun safety — in the home and on the range — as well as basic marksmanship. The legal aspects of handgun use will be explained in some form of personal protection course. You will probably not get any defensive handgun training at this level other than firing from a supported position, such as resting the gun on a table or shooting bench, and possibly at the five-yard limit, standing erect, firing the gun supported by both hands.

One benefit is that you'll meet like-minded people with whom you might develop a rapport and then have someone with whom to start to practice. The instructor and others at the gun club can also direct you toward other self-defense courses. If you join the NRA, you will also be assured of a continuing supply of timely, valid firearms information. Other NRA benefits include firearms theft insurance and a means to locate safe places to shoot.

(You do intend to insure your firearm and you do want a place to shoot and someone with whom to share your interests, don't you?)

The NRA course fees are generally quite reasonable and most of the instructors have, at the very least, an adequate knowledge of firearms. Many of them are very knowledgeable.

OK, you're already past all this. You want to know exactly what will increase your "survival quotient." Where do you go and what should you do?

Going, doing and learning are only limited by your available time and the content of your wallet. As of this writing, I've located about 80 defensive shooting schools in the USA. Added to this, most every commercial firing range and many private clubs have local instructors who teach some form of firearm shooting skills and self-defense. (They range from abysmally atrocious to world-class excellent.)

Going forward from the basics, I would strongly recommend getting professional instruction right from the start. Learn the right way before you have a bunch of bad habits to break.

As far as which school to attend, as more states have passed reasonable laws for obtaining concealed weapons permits, it seems as if there is a new defensive shooting school cropping up somewhere each week. Sorting through them is a full-time job. Not a few of these schools claim to teach the "secrets of the Ninja gunfighters" to hook you into coming to their school. Fortunately, market place economics (read "they are incompetent") drive most of them out of business.

If you're in law enforcement, training opportunities are virtually unlimited. There's the Federal Law Enforcement Training Center in Glynco, Georgia; the FBI and DEA at Quantico, VA; and the US Secret Service, all great places to learn firearms and other defensive techniques. The FBI also hosts regional training for law enforcement officers. Most times, all it takes is a call from the Chief of Police to the organization and a spot will be found in an upcoming class. In addition, Heckler & Koch, Smith & Wesson, Sigarms and Glock all offer firearms training for the LE professional. (Smith & Wesson also offers civilian firearms training.)

If you're an unsworn civilian, the options are just as good as for the cops. To find a good school or a good instructor, I would go with word-of-mouth recommendations from one or two shooters who have been to some private academies and whose opinion you respect. In other words, before spending time and money, get some references and know what you're getting into at any one school.

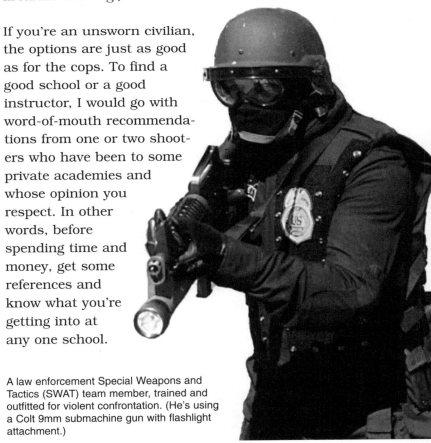

A law enforcement Special Weapons and Tactics (SWAT) team member, trained and outfitted for violent confrontation. (He's using a Colt 9mm submachine gun with flashlight attachment.)

80

Just because I happen to be enamored of Clint Smith's Thunder Ranch fighting school in Texas doesn't mean you'll share the same evaluation. But I do think Clint Smith and his staff are tops at teaching you how to survive lethal armed conflict. They don't care about making you the local "top gun" at a club match; that's not what they're about. They teach you how to **fight**. Another good choice is the Gunsite Training Center in Arizona, whose curriculum covers the same defensive skills package. Both are excellent and are, deservedly, the top two nationally-recognized fighting schools in the USA.

If you can afford it, attending a formal training school such as Thunder Ranch, shown here, is money well spent.

Of course, there are other great defensive-training firearms instructors out there. I can personally recommend John Farnum's Defensive Tactics Institute and Massad Ayoob's Lethal Force Institute, as well as Jim Cirillo's classes. I have also heard very good things about the Front Sight training school run by Naish Piazza, as well as Chuck Taylor's school.

Some firearms instructors, who are more than qualified to teach defensive shooting skills, shy away from doing so for fear of legal repercussions if the student screws up his real-life exam and is involved in a "bad" shooting. These latter instructors teach Practical Shooting competition skills used in the International Practical Shooting Confederation (IPSC) action shooting game. Wait. Don't tune out, saying that competition is not your cup of tea. You asked for someplace to learn self-defense skills. Well, part of self-defense is total proficiency in the *dynamic use* of firearms. (And, in truth, some of these instructors are teaching competitive shooting skills based on their lawyer's advice to steer clear of any defense instruction.)

Practical Shooting competition often requires shooting both steel and paper targets.

Competition training is a more emotionally-comfortable way to acquire your gun handling skills, for there is very little talk of life-taking but rather the competitors discuss how to win at the game. Many of the shooting techniques are the same for competition or defense, of course — center hits win! The difference is in the application. The competition schools will teach you how to shoot extremely well. They won't address when to shoot or what your actions should be when facing a threat. These learned practical shooting skills are most often acquired for IPSC sporting competition, which is run under the auspices of the United States Practical Shooting Association (USPSA), which organizes and administers local, regional and national competition. In the USA, IPSC/USPSA also offers a basic gun handling/safety course for new member competitors, but this is a verification of acquired skills, not a training class.

The Advanced Tactical Group (ATG) has found that scenario training exercises are the definitive test of acquired defensive skills. (Shown: ATG personnel conducting such exercises at the US Secret Service Regional Pistol Match in 1995.)

The International Defensive Pistol Association (IDPA) offers more realistic practical shooting competition and is an organized venue where you can get some "real-world" practice in a competitive format. In addition, going to IPSC and IDPA matches is a good place to find like-minded people. (Certainly better than hanging around a gun store and the "wannabes" that frequent many of them.)

Earlier, I mentioned Massad Ayoob and his Lethal Force Institute (LFI). This school emphasizes the what, why and how of the confrontation and the personal and legal repercussions that result therefrom and, in addition, provides basic defensive-handgun skills. LFI has a large curriculum from very basic to extremely advanced training in self-defense and is not limited to firearms. Alternative self-defense tactics instruction in less-than-lethal weapons is also taught.

Which course of action is best for you? You won't go wrong going to any or all of the schools as your finances permit. You may well learn more at one than at the next, of course, depending on how the instructors relate to you and vice versa. Unfortunately, every self-defense gun buyer wants the knowledge, but not many are willing — or able — to spend the tuition, travel and expense money for a week's education at one of these fine schools. (And one week will not a gunfighter make.)

It's curious but human nature, I guess, that a person will spend $500 to $2,000 on a gun and another $100+ on accessories and then want to find someone or someplace to learn for free. But in shooting, as in every other aspect of life, you get what you pay for. A few thousand dollars spent on training is a cheap insurance premium.

OK. You don't want to do any of the above. You simply

want to learn by yourself, away from others and without drawing any attention to your interest in personal protection. Understandable, but the most difficult path to excellence.

I would suggest the following: Start by becoming as familiar with the handgun as you are with your knife and fork. After making sure the gun is empty, carry it around with you every waking moment of your day and take it to bed with you. Use a holster, practice your draw and also carry it in your hand at times. If you put it down for any reason, clear it to insure that it's unloaded *each and every time* you pick it up. Yes, this is a very repetitious drill. Yes, checking the gun each time is possibly excessive. But if you do this for a week or so, you **will** be safety conscious and you **will** know the gun. (The military — in my time, at least — was very good at this. We *lived* with our M-1 rifles for our entire basic training cycle.)

While you're doing all this toting and checking, you should also dry fire at a designated target. (Dry firing is done after *double checking* that the gun is unloaded.) You

Your eyes focus on the front sight, while your designated target is blurred in the background.

pick the target. I'd recommend a reduced-silhouette target. Draw and "click" at it with one hand and two-hand supported and then with your "off" hand, again one- or two-handed. And don't neglect "moving" targets, either. Aim at the end of a window shade cord that's swaying in the breeze, for example, or some leaves that are being blown around your yard. (**Do not use live targets!** Never cover anything with your gun muzzle that you are not willing to destroy!!)

NOTE: During this period of familiarization, I strongly recommend that you lock up or put away any ammunition that might fit in the gun. If you start loading the gun when you think you might need it and then unload it for the "walk around," you **will** eventually get the sequence backwards.

One very critical area that needs to be examined is the modification or customizing of a gun for defensive use. Do we need to do it? What are the customizing or modifications that are almost always done and recommended for the defensive handgun? Chapter Eight will answer those questions and more.

In Chapter 10, we'll cover practice, training and proficiency, including various types of organized shooting disciplines and their efficacy toward self-defense training. Then we'll provide some suggested individual practice drills.

CHAPTER 8

TO CUSTOMIZE OR NOT TO CUSTOMIZE

W e're all unique in ourselves, lone identities among all other human beings. When we're lumped in with the rest of the world, we rebel in one fashion or another to reassert our individuality (teenagers are a prime example of this), so changing or customizing our firearms is not in the least extraordinary behavior. Hell, even the American Indians hammered copper and iron nails into their gun stocks to individualize them.

Browning High Power in 9x19mm, customized by pistolsmith Richard Heinie.

As the proud owner of quite a few custom combat handguns, I must admit that the plethora of articles written on the inadvisability of using a custom gun for self-defense disturbs me. I surely won't stop carrying a customized gun, but I've seen others who have become very radical on the matter. One guy I know first put all his customized (twenty-some) handguns in his safe and then went out and bought factory stock replacements for every one of them so that he would have lawyer-proof handguns to carry. I think this is nuts!

In particular, my friend Massad Ayoob has written extensively on the pitfalls of custom guns and exotic ammunition and I was under the distinct impression that he was the origin and source of the "don't use a custom gun or the lawyers will get you" syndrome. Fortunately, I sent this manuscript to Mas for his opinion and advice. He quickly corrected my impression and pointed out a few things. First, he carries custom guns most all the time. (True. I've always seen him with one nice custom gun or another.) Second, when he wrote about the bogeyman custom gun stuff, he was quoting "learned counsel," a trial lawyer who very strongly advised against using a custom gun for self-defense.

Another Browning High Power in 9x19mm, this one customized by pistolsmith Wayne Novak.

As things go, Mas, as the messenger, has taken the heat for advice passed on to him by a well-respected lawyer experienced on firearms matters in civil and criminal court. Mas has tried, in good faith, to do a service for gun owners who might use a firearm to defend themselves. It obviously hasn't worked out all that well, for he now has the reputation of being against custom guns and nothing could be further from the truth.

Be this as it may, what has developed is something I term the "Ayoob Syndrome," in that there are now many gun owners who are petrified of changing anything on a new handgun, regardless of the real need, for fear of what questions they might be asked in court.

A little rational thought is in order to counter this "don't use a custom handgun or the lawyer-bogeyman will get you" stuff. I continue to carry my custom Swenson .45s for self-defense because they are exquisite tools for the job. However, you do need to evaluate the gun you're going to be toting and potentially using, for when and if you do engage Mr. Bad Guy, the authorities will take your handgun and securely lock it away for a very long time, if not forever. You may well never see your $3000 custom handgun again after firing one shot — or even

A customized Para-Ordnance in .45ACP done by Mike LaRocca.

none. I admit that, more and more, I leave the Swensons at home. They're just too damned nice to give up!

Will a custom gun hurt you in legal proceedings? Yes and no. Yes in civil cases and no in criminal ones, but not always and it depends.

The judicial system is a law unto itself and anything can happen. (For instance, look at some of the more high-profile murderers who have escaped justice.) I find that in general, in a criminal case, the judge and jury want to know who shot the guy, why was he shot and did he deserve it. I've not found that the criminal case judge was so sloppy that he let a prosecutor discuss those matters which did not speak directly to the crime of who, why and was it justified. (But yes, the court does allow questions such as, "Why did you shoot him so many times?")

If a firearm is used, the ballistics lab will examine the handgun and render a report that says, in essence, this is an X-brand five-shot blued-steel revolver, .22LR caliber, barrel length 2", with a double-action trigger pull of 12 pounds and a single-action pull of six pounds. The

A well-carried standard Colt .380 Government Model semi-automatic pistol.

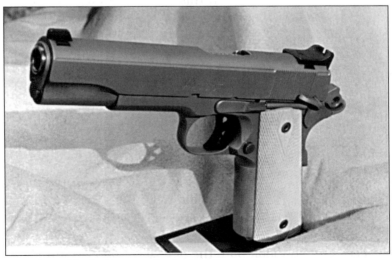
A Colt Delta Elite in 10mm, customized by Phoenix Armory.

revolver contained five spent X-brand casings which are similar to brand-X bullets. The report will then point out that the five brand-X bullets in the deceased's body and supplied to the lab match the rifling characteristics of test bullets fired from this revolver and the whole report will be "State's Exhibit Number 1."

The prosector might say something about a hair trigger — once, but a competent judge isn't going to let him tip-toe down this path any farther. The weight of the trigger pull doesn't speak to the offense, unless the defense is claiming an accidental discharge. (This is where the defense team brings in its firearms expert witness to counterbalance the prosecution's statements and witnesses.)

I'm not a lawyer, but given this direction of a criminal case, you can fairly readily see what's going to be "let in" and what is not.

In a civil case, however, what Mas reported is much more on point. The plaintiff's lawyer, representing the poor needy family of the deceased, can get away with much, much more in his questioning. As my friend and retired Philadelphia Police Officer Roger Tucker observed dryly, "There's nothing like the killing of a man to make him a saint." The plaintiff's lawyer is going to ask you the most outrageous questions on so many matters that it will appear that *you* are on trial and not the deceased. That's his job. (And you *are* on trial.) If the plaintiff's lawyer is successful, you look bad, the deceased looks "saintly" and the jury gives your (or the insurance company's) money away.

Yes, you can use a factory-stock gun to deflect some of this line of questioning. You can make sure you don't use

a Colt Combat Elite, Combat Government or a Colt
Cobra, a Smith & Wesson Combat Masterpiece (S&W
Model 15) or Combat Magnum (S&W Model 19). Also,
skip over the Charter Arms Bulldog or Pug revolvers and
get something "safe," say a Jennings, Bryco, Lorcin or a
Phoenix. Of course, these are all inexpensively-made
handguns and when Mr. Lawyer isn't torturing you about
the combat guns, he'll get on you for using a "cheap"
gun. The point is, most anything you do can be twisted to
make you look wrong or portray you in a poor light.

The jury is, fortunately, the wild card in all this. In most
criminal cases, they can see through the BS and decide if
the guy needed killing, regardless of the tools used. This
doesn't mean, however, that you will be acquitted. The
jury may feel that some punishment is merited.
Conversely, in a civil trial, they might just decide that the
very attractive, grieving widow with her six kids needs
some money from someone and you're the luckless but
monied soul in the dock. If this happens, you flat-out lose
— and there's not a damned thing you can do about it!

The question remains: what constitutes a custom gun?
You can lawyer this a bit yourself by playing "what if."
What if you change the grips so that you can hang onto
the gun when you practice with it or change the sights so
that you can aim more accurately? What if you checker
the gripstraps and install an extended beavertail for better recoil control? At what point do modifications become
customizing? Everyone is really just playing with words
here. Any change to a standard product can be considered customizing. Hence my friend's storage of his modi-
fied guns and the buying of all new standard guns. He
carried the subject through to its logical end.

If you carry gun modifications out logically, as my friend with the twenty-some guns did, you'll never change anything on your self-defense gun just so you won't have the tricky "gun questions" asked of you if you're ever forced to use it. Of course, if you don't make needed modifications, you may not be able to use it effectively, for guns are designed to fit everyone "sort of." Therefore, they fit no one "exactly" without some modifications. (Much like a man's suit. Rarely does a suit fit right off the rack. It usually needs some alterations to fit properly.)

Let's take a typical revolver buyer, for example. He (or she) decides a double-action revolver is the more simple of the two handgun types to operate. Right off, the revolver may feel uncomfortable in the buyer's hands. Naturally, the firearms dealer is more than willing to help by selling the buyer a pair of aftermarket grips that change the "feel" of the gun.

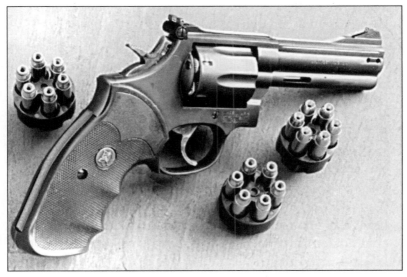

This Smith & Wesson L-frame .357 Magnum revolver, highly-customized by Phoenix Armory, is an excellent defense gun.

Next, the buyer might find that the double action is difficult to operate. No problem; simply replace the springs with an aftermarket set of lighter springs from an aftermarket spring kit supplier. Viola! The action is now easier to operate. But the buyer has customized his gun twice and now has, according to the "no customizing" argument, two strikes against him. And he hasn't even decided on his defense ammunition yet.

If Mr. Self-defense goes instead with a semi-auto pistol of any type and changes the sights and grips, he could well be asked, "Why isn't a revolver good enough for your defense. Why do you need a gun that shoots so fast and holds so many rounds and why did you need to further modify this killing machine?" (Starting to see how you're "damned if you do, damned if you don't"?)

This standard 1911 semi-auto Llama is inexpensive yet effective.

Also, if you buy and use state-of-the-art ammunition, you can be portrayed as having selected the most devastating rounds which you deliberately intended to use on Mr. Bad Guy. "What was wrong with using the standard generic ammo?," you could be asked. One excellent answer is, "I bought and use the same ammunition as is used by police departments throughout the United States."

All this discussion about names, action types and modification to your firearm and we haven't even gotten into your "extensive" or "inadequate" amount of firearms training and practice.

Yes, your *training* can easily be made an issue. Not the lack of, but that you *made the effort* to get good training. You can be portrayed as a wannabe killer for spending a week and $2000 getting great firearms instruction at Thunder Ranch. The lawyer might very well make the statement that just going to a local club instructor for training wasn't good enough, *you* wanted to be a "gunfighter" and were just itching for an excuse to use your new-found skills on his client.

Oh, and don't forget, you can worry yourself sick over the name of the holster you use, too. Are you carrying your gun in a Pro Fed? Must be a closet cop imitator. Are you wearing an Askins Avenger? This could easily lead to some really sarcastic comments in court. If this logic is followed out, you'll only wear Uncle Mike's holsters — unless the case can be made that you are parent-deprived, thus mentally unstable and needed a surrogate Uncle figure to support your damaged psyche. (Actually, in this age of the "abuse excuse," this might be a good defense for you.)

All this quibbling about changes and how they are going to be seen is like arguing with your spouse. No matter

what you do or say, it can be twisted so as to make you look bad. If the point of the selected gun, ammo and holster is to save your life or protect others, why wouldn't you make

The Smith & Wesson Model 625, a modern version of the large-frame S&W .45ACP-chambered revolver.

damned sure you've got the very best tools?

There *is* a middle ground for gun modifications. Do only those modifications which enhance your ability to use the arm effectively, *without eliminating any safety features.* This will minimize your potential legal exposure and discomfort on the witness stand or in depositions. (Mas Ayoob has also written this advice in his discussions, but the point is often overlooked during the onset of the resulting paranoia.) One good guide is to say to yourself, "If it isn't broken, don't fix it." If your gun of choice does everything that you ask of it, leave it alone.

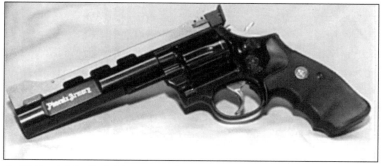

A .38 Special Smith & Wesson revolver, customized by Phoenix Armory for police competition shooting.

If you just have the urge to try out different alterations or gadgets, save the project gun for use at the range. In truth, you probably know what are reasonable changes and modifications and what are not. (I know, what's reasonable to you and me may well not be to the jury. No one ever said the law was fair.) For me, an example of a stupid change would be a 1.5-pound trigger pull weight on my 1911 single-action .45 semi-auto. This is not a carry trigger — for me. I'm sure that a world-class IPSC shooter could make a good case to himself and also to the court for using this light a trigger.

In my opinion, changing grips, sights, accurizing, checkering, smoothing out trigger pulls, getting more visible aftermarket sights (including night sights), refinishing and adding or modifying parts (such as a wider beavertail on a 1911 or Browning High Power) to aid in recoil control are all eminently practical custom changes that I'm comfortable defending in court for myself or anyone else.

"Defending in court" is the crux of the matter, of course. Both sides dig up their version of a gun expert, whom they ensure is going to testify to exactly those points that strengthen their case. You wind up with a swearing contest between expert witnesses. The jury usually looks at both sides and discounts both sides' expert testimony — unless it's very accurate on the one side and patently false on the other.

At this point, you say you can't afford the experts. Well, you should consider the real cost of defending your actions in court and being acquitted. (This is not "found innocent" — just "acquitted." The jury doesn't say you're innocent. Just that the facts were not enough to convict you of the crime charged.)

When, not if, you are arrested for shooting Mr. Bad Guy, the whole thing from arrest to acquittal should cost you anywhere from $25,000 to $75,000 — and you probably won't get your gun back, either. That being the case, I think it is much more important to consider how you're going to pay for your defense, rather than concern yourself with what the prosecutor will say about your ivory grips. (This subject is covered in greater detail in the next chapter.)

CHAPTER 9

THE AFTERMATH

OK, you've defended hearth and home or you've overcome a deadly-force attack and the attacker is now dead. What happens next? Nothing pleasant. You are now in a deep world of trouble — both legal and personal. Cynically put, it might have been better to have been robbed, raped or beaten.

Legally, you have killed. The authorities don't know if it was justified homicide or premeditated murder. You may have (only) committed manslaughter, voluntary or involuntary. I'm not a lawyer and don't intend to beat this to death with a bunch of legal terms. Suffice to say that no law enforcement agency is going to view you as a hero. You are a suspect and, in almost all cases, considered guilty until proven otherwise.

This is a **given**. The authorities will be more than glad to listen to and record your side of the events. Telling your side of the story is not a wise thing to do, though, without your lawyer present, since the cops' job is to find the guilt of the person who brought the harm to the other person (the deceased). Law enforcement, in theory, looks equally at the guilt or innocence of the suspect, but their job is to gather all the facts and circumstances of the occurrence with the intent of prosecution. This information goes to the District Attorney's office, which will then determine if you should be tried in a court of law.

Now, let's stop and think about this a bit. Let's create a simple scenario. You're awakened to the sound of your front door being broken in. You grab a firearm, a telephone, a flashlight and whatever else comes to mind. A shape looms in your bedroom door. You shoot and the shape falls to the floor. You turn on the lights and see that the shape has the form of the neighbors' 15-year-old daughter. Oops!!

The police have already arrived. The girl is very dead and you have the gun at your side. Now, just what is the officer going to do? Note the broken door? Note your frantic 911 emergency call, call the Coroner's Office to have the body removed and then say to you, "Have a nice night."? Not hardly. Sure, I'm exaggerating a bit. It could just be a neighbor's 15-year-old son. We can embellish this a bit with the details that come out during the investigation. He's been diagnosed as a "gifted" child and is dysfunctional in school. He's been a problem in the neighborhood, playing his stereo loudly and generally raising hell. You know him, because you've made complaints about him to the police in the past, as have your neighbors. But they haven't killed him, you have. The question arises, "Why did you shoot?" The police will ask you that and you damned well better not answer without the advice of your lawyer.

Believe me: There is **no** political prosecutorial entity that is not going to have you indicted for this killing. You will have to prove your innocence by showing fear of extreme bodily harm, coupled with not recognizing that the intruder was only "a child" and your lack of ability to retreat or to control the problem with less-than-lethal force. Until you can do that, you are going to be presumed to be guilty of one of the legal definitions of homicide until proven otherwise.

"Proven otherwise" translates into arrest, inquest, grand jury indictment and trial. All these matters are conducted in a court of law, so that means lawyer time. Privately-retained lawyers get big bucks for representing those who have killed. An hourly rate of $175 to $250 is not out of line, plus paralegal and administrative costs. In fact, a good criminal defense lawyer will ask for, in advance, at least $1000 to represent you at the preliminary hearing. After the hearing, he'll establish a substantially higher fee ($25,000 or more) to continue with the case up to any trial. You may not need to come up with the entire $25,000 at once, but he'll want some real money in hand and some very good assurance of the remainder.

Court-appointed public defender attorneys are "free," but you have to be broke before you can get one. By the way, the private lawyer may not be as able to represent you as the PD, who gets many more such cases during a year. Of course, the PD's office is overworked in large cities, so you can lose big-time this way, too.

Now you have already been arrested, processed and put into the county prison. The next hurdle is bail. Can you get out of jail before the trial? I'm working on the assumption that it's a fairly clear-cut case of self-defense (preferably on videotape), coupled with a local District Attorney who's not running for re-election and isn't anti-gun, and the guy you killed isn't "different" enough from you to raise the voices of various "Cause" groups. If all these circumstances prevail, you will *probably* be granted bail at a bail hearing (requiring an additional attorney fee, of course). How you get out of prison varies from county to county and from state to state and also depends on the charges filed against you. Sometimes, a charge of premeditated murder is not bailable. This means you remain in custody until trial.

If you are afforded bail, sometimes the state will require cash or property-equivalent ranging from $25,000 to $1,000,000 before they let you out. A bail bondsman charges 10% (or higher) of the face amount of the bail and you don't get his percentage back. You usually wind up putting your home up as collateral.

Now, back to the attorney. He'll most likely want a fee in the range of $25,000 to $50,000 to represent you during the trial. (This is *in addition to* the first $25,000.) At this point, you're probably saying to yourself that you don't have that kind of money. Sure you do. You, or your wife with power of attorney, gets a second mortgage on your home and starts to sell off or convert your assets into cash.

Your job? Well again, depending on the notoriety of the incident, you don't have one anymore. (And you probably won't qualify for unemployment compensation, either.)

Wait, there's more. Before you even get to the lawyer and bail stage, the police will most assuredly ask if you have a handgun carry permit and do you own any other guns. (They will check their files, as well.) The permit *will* get cancelled and the cops will come and confiscate the gun(s), preferably with a court order, but not always. (You just killed someone, so obviously you shouldn't have access to firearms.) You can't legally carry a gun, if you had one, and if you're out on bail and indicted, you also can't buy or be in possession of a firearm or ammunition. (You should check the current BATF rules.)

Now, if the afore-mentioned District Attorney is all the things that you don't want him to be, there will be press conferences, particularly if you own more than two or three guns. The DA and the press can talk about your "arsenal," which will be prominently displayed for the camera. And, of course, you, or at least your photo, will be on the 6 O'Clock News. You will personally get to meet those talking heads from the TV stations, as well as every other press-type, as they jam their microphones and cameras in your face when you come out of court. If you have shot one of the poor unfortunates of our society, you'll probably have demonstrators outside your home along with the camera crews.

Leave town? Not likely. Your passport will be confiscated and your travel restricted to the state in which you live, with any other travel to be approved by the court. Welcome to the world of the accused.

Now, let's stipulate (one of those nice "lawyer" terms) that you've gotten a lawyer, made bail and are now going to trial. First off, most DAs are going to offer you a "deal," otherwise known as a plea bargain. He'll offer to reduce the charges and time in the hoosegow in return for a plea of guilty. Sometimes the deal is very good, with charges being dropped all the way down to a misdemeanor offense that bears no resemblance to the details of the actual occurrence. Your lawyer will also probably tell you to

Your view at the moment of confrontation!

103

take the best deal you can. If you do, that may be it for **ever** getting near a gun or holding a decent job again.

You're innocent, so you decide on a trial.

One of the greatest misconceptions held by the American public is that you are innocent until proven guilty in a court of law. Quite the contrary. You will have to — must — prove your innocence to be found not guilty. This finding of "not guilty," by the way, does not mean that you were found innocent. It just says that there was not a body of evidence strong enough to convince a jury beyond a reasonable doubt that you committed the crime for which you had been charged. Nice, huh?

OK, you've been acquitted, found not guilty of all charges. The ordeal is over, right? Wrong! Now it's time for phase two of your travails. The deceased's relatives or some other entity which has "standing" (another legal term) in the matter now enters a civil lawsuit against you. No problem, you think; you've already been acquitted. But that was in a criminal court. Civil proceedings have a different standard of proof. Now all that is needed to convict you is a *preponderance* of evidence, not evidence beyond a reasonable doubt. Translated, this means that if there is 50.0001% of the evidence sufficient to show that you should be found guilty, you are so found. The plaintiff then moves for monetary damages, which translates into "they want everything you have (left)." It helps if you have homeowner's insurance that specifically covers an overt injurious act. Most homeowner's policies cover accidents, not deliberate acts, but with some shopping you may be able to get a policy that will cover you for actively shooting an intruder.

As the civil phase develops and your insurance company becomes involved, the company may well settle

out of court with the plaintiff. (A civil form of the same plea bargaining that happens in criminal trials.) This deal-making has nothing to do with your guilt or innocence. The insurance company just figures out which is cheaper, a trial or a settlement. They then go for the lesser amount. You have nothing to say in this matter. (Read the fine print in your homeowner's policy.)

The "bad guy's" view at the moment of confrontation!

Of course, when the insurance company settles out of court, everyone in the world will now be convinced that you did do what the headlines said you did and the settlement was just to avoid the bigger penalty you would have gotten when you were convicted in the civil case. This means those who sort of considered you innocent up through and after the criminal trial will now be convinced that you were really guilty of the criminal charges and just "got off" due to a slick lawyer. (You will also find out very quickly who your friends are.)

Anyway, now everything is settled. You're a free man. You now have no money, large mortgage(s), no job and no friends. (And possibly no family, either, for the strain of a criminal and/or civil trial is devastating to relationships.)

You also don't have any of your guns back. That requires a separate court hearing and judicial order. The judge might well not grant you your property back and then you will have to appeal this, too. That means back to the lawyer who filed the appeal in the first place. If you complain to the authorities about all that has transpired, they'll simply point out that the system worked. All the facts and circumstances were examined and you were found not guilty by a jury of your peers.

You can now see why it might be better not to shoot but to retreat, avoid, escape or take the assault. Medical and other insurance will cover you — as long as you don't die — and you've got insurance for that, too. Life-taking really is a last resort!

Footnote: Yes, this is a very cynical, jaundiced presentation of the US legal system. But it's a real view. However, the US justice system is still the best in the world. It is much worse in other countries.

CHAPTER 10

PRACTICE, TRAINING AND PROFICIENCY

There must be an understanding of the difference between training, practice and proficiency so that the student of self-defense can better focus on his goals.

Training is formal or informal instruction where you are shown concepts and techniques. *Practice* is just that — where you work at perfecting what you have been taught after the block of instruction is complete. *Proficiency* is how you grade yourself or are graded — by your own standards, in competition or in an actual life-threatening encounter.

The beginning student of self-defense should, if at all possible, get the best-qualified instruction to save time, money and, more important, avoid developing bad habits that will be difficult if not impossible to discard. As I mentioned earlier, the National Rifle Association offers very good basic courses on firearms that include the safe handling of guns and their use in home, personal defense and competition. Many gun clubs and commercial ranges offer similar courses typically titled "Personal Protection," or some variation thereof. The quality and content of the NRA courses is uniformly good. The other courses range from very good to horrid, depending on the quality of the instructor. It is all too easy to find a "wannabe commando" offering some sort of self-defense training.

In the realm of alternative self-defense courses (other than those taught by the NRA), there are approximately 80 shooting/defensive firearms schools advertising their services in the USA. I only have good feedback on a few of them, as I mentioned in Chapter 7. The first modern school for firearms — and possibly the best known — is the Gunsite Training Center in Paulden, Arizona. Founded by Col. Jeff Cooper in the mid-1970s as the American Pistol Institute, it was the benchmark against which all other schools of its ilk were measured. I've been to the "new" Gunsite ("new" in that Col. Cooper no longer owns it nor teaches there) on four occasions, but haven't attended any of the instruction. While I was there and had the opportunity to observe classes in progress, I noted that the instructors were top-notch and totally dedicated to providing the very best training to their students. Being a "Gunsite Graduate" is viewed by attendees as a badge of honor and a statement of their firearms proficiency.

Clint Smith, left, explains the proper use of a rifle for a house clearing during an Urban Rifle Course at Thunder Ranch.

Clint Smith, far left, discusses proper technique with students during a Home and Vehicle Defense Course at Thunder Ranch.

The most modern of the current fighting schools is Thunder Ranch, Inc. run by Clint Smith in Mountain Home, Texas. This multi-million dollar operation has the best facilities and attracts and keeps the best of the cadre of professional firearms instructors. I've been to Thunder Ranch on at least four occasions and have attended classes in Home and Vehicle Defense, a pistol course; Urban Rifle, which teaches fighting with a rifle at handgun distances; and H.I.T. (High Intensity Tactical), a high-speed, low-drag overview of defensive skills using a handgun. There is nothing negative that I can say about Thunder Ranch — not its staff instructors nor the facilities. Every instructor at the Ranch knows his stuff and teaches it so that it is easily understood and retained.

Other academies worth attending are the S&W Academy in Springfield, Massachusetts, under the able direction of Robert Hunt (Lt. Col., Ret., MA State Police) and the HK International Training Center in Chantilly, Virginia, directed by John Myer. Sigarms also has an outstanding firearms training staff, as does Glock. While HK, Glock and Sigarms only teach law enforcement personnel, S&W now has civilian-focused instruction taught by the same high-quality law enforcement instructors.

Any of these schools will more than suffice to start you on the correct path to developing and maintaining life-saving self-defense skills. I recommend them all without reservation. But as a caution, I would strongly suggest getting numerous references from graduates of any of the lesser-known schools you're considering before spending time and money. There are as many charlatans in the firearms field as there are in any other commercial endeavor. And another caution: Note I said "*start* you on the correct path." Just taking a week-long course doesn't finish your education and training. It is merely a means to get the solid building blocks upon which you construct your self-defense wall.

The Advanced Tactical Group (ATG) tailors instruction to fit particular needs; in this case, executive protection.

To determine your proficiency before or after attending a school, there are, as I mentioned before, organized firearms competitions that will validate your acquired skills...or show you where your weaknesses are. For instance, if you shoot formal NRA pistol competition, you'll learn and practice the fundamentals of excellent marksmanship, for the competition is fired one-handed at bullseyes, usually in three stages of slow, timed and rapid fire. The first stage is ten shots in five or ten minutes, then two runs of five shots in twenty seconds each and finally two five-shot strings in ten seconds each. This competition rewards extremely precise and methodical shooting techniques. This venue has no defensive coloring and is generally viewed as a recreational activity that will offend very few.

If you elect to try Practical Pistol Shooting administered under the auspices of IPSC/USPSA, your proficiency in drawing from a holster and being able to engage multiple humanoid targets with one or two rounds will be developed. IPSC shooting problems reward those whose skills permit them to shoot their handgun with a moderate amount of accuracy but with great speed, both from a fixed position and while moving from shooting point to shooting point. IPSC had its origins in realistic defensive handgun use; however, the emphasis has now shifted to a dynamic but sporting use of handguns. As this discipline has evolved into a full-fledged "sport," trick guns, holsters and ammunition have become the norm, rather

The author, firing in a national Practical Shooting competition.

than ordinary, out-of-the-box handguns, although IPSC does retain a division in which users of lesser-customized guns and holsters can still compete.

The International Defensive Pistol Association (IDPA) supports more realistic courses of fire, mandates the use of ordinary, non-exotic handguns and is a better venue for the self-defense-oriented shooter.

Other offshoots of Practical Shooting can be found in bowling pin shoots and steel plate shoots. These competitions are good for developing gun handling and shooting skills and many find them less competitively-intensive than IPSC. In the "pin" shoots, the challenge, starting with your gun in hand, is to knock five to nine bowling pins off a table 15 yards or so down range. Pin shooting has some real-life application because the bowling pins require solid hits with a center-fire handgun to get them off the table. (The bowling pin, coincidentally, is just about the size of the "kill" zone on the average person.) "Steel" shoots are more shooting-arcade-type games, since the steel plates used can be tipped over with almost any center-fire handgun. Steel and pin shooting teach fast and accurate shooting on small, multiple targets, and are great fun. Another advantage of bowling pin and steel contests is that they often have shotgun shoots against the same pins and steel. This gives you a chance to do some work with your shotgun, but avoids a self-defense connotation.

The goals in these competitive events are obviously not the life-saving goals learned at the shooting academies, but they do offer an opportunity for dynamic gun handling under the artificial stress of a competitive environment. Many winning skills in these sports have crossover application to self-defense techniques; for instance, rapidly engaging multiple targets, firing on the move and shooting from constrained positions such as over or under barricades. However, some of the other winning skills run exactly *opposite* to trying to stay alive. One egregious example: in IPSC/USPSA Practical Shooting matches, the competitors will engage targets without seeking protective cover and reload on the run, again exposed, and with no regard for unused cartridges discarded along with the magazine. In self-defense training, of course, cover should be used whenever possible and discarding ammunition is obviously not a good technique.

Cover should always be used if readily available.

If organized competition doesn't appeal to you, with a little effort you should be able to find a few small, unaffiliated groups in your area who practice self-defense shooting skills in scenario formats that adhere to more realistic tactical doctrine yet are not allied with any national organization. Their focus is on improving their own defensive techniques and not winning shooting games. One drawback to these groups is they don't progress much due to lack of fresh, outside input because they tend to degenerate into a "good old boys" shooting and socializing club. Or, more frighteningly, they migrate toward a "militia" mentality. (There are a number of states which prohibit groups from banding together to practice "survival" skills.)

Of course, getting good formal training is expensive and not everyone can afford the money or time needed — but they still have a very real and pressing need to develop at least some basic handgun skills for self-defense. With these limitations in mind, I suggest the following training regime:

If you're the average person looking to defend yourself with a gun, you must first learn to handle it safely. This should entail at least taking the previously-mentioned NRA Personal Protection Course. You must be able to load, unload, clean and store your firearm and know how to safely and effectively carry it on your person. You most assuredly want to know the law as to when, where and how you can use the gun in self-defense, which is best learned from a practicing criminal-law attorney. Next, you want to be able shoot it accurately, but you're most likely not interested in becoming a world-class pistolero. You just want to get your shots on target at reasonable distances.

Author's wife instructing friend Sandy Kuritzky in basic pistol skills. (Proper instruction in the safe handling of firearms is a must!)

If these are your parameters, I recommend that you begin training and practice with a revolver and only use a semi-auto pistol if you're totally comfortable with this type of handgun action. Then shoot only at close range — the target positioned at three feet (as close as a normal conversation) — and never any further away from you than five yards for most of your practice. If five yards sounds too close, consider that this is 15 feet — more than the length of the average interior room with furniture in it and about two car-lengths in distance. Yes, you should include some practice at farther distances (10, 15, 20 and 25 yards), but the consensus is that the large majority of confrontations take place at arm's length. The bad guy needs to be close enough to you to talk to you and to remove whatever it is he wants from you. He's going to have a hard time doing that at 15, 20 or 25 yards.

Start your practice regimen standing erect with both eyes open and holding the gun with one or two hands. Your gun arm should be fully extended, centered on your nose, and held in a direct line from your face to the target. This is the most natural means of holding a handgun (like pointing your finger at something). Your hand or hands must do a few things to and for the gun. The gun must stay directed at the target and you must hold it firmly enough to keep it from bouncing around in your hand(s) when it's fired, as well as to give enough resistance to the recoil so that you can quickly realign the gun on the same or additional targets if additional shots are needed.

If all this sounds too simple, well, self-defense shooting should be simple. Self-defense practice is as simple. Most of us just make it unnecessarily complex. Your only self-defense goal is to get hits on target in the easiest, most natural manner possible. "Looking good" doesn't count for spit if you die.

IMPORTANT NOTE: ALL OF THE FOLLOWING EXERCISES SHOULD FIRST BE PRACTICED WITH AN UNLOADED FIREARM!

Naturally stand erect. Naturally hold the gun out in front of you with both hands. Naturally lean forward slightly, for you're going to have a gun recoiling in your hands when it fires. This is where most folks get messed up. They lean backward to counterbalance the weight of the gun, so when it goes off and recoils in their hands, they're pushed farther backward, off balance. You can easily experience this without firing a gun. Have someone push against your two hands while they're clasped together (without a gun in them, of course) and extended out in front of you. They'll be pushing you backward, off balance. Now lean forward and you'll see that they can't unbalance you.

Naturally point the gun at where you want the bullet to go. Use the sights to verify that you're pointing the gun correctly. Pull the trigger with a firm, sure movement as you look at the target with the gun in your peripheral vision. At these close distances, your trigger finger can be on the trigger as far as the first joint. (Yes, target and competition shooters use the pad of their trigger finger for a more-precise trigger movement, but attempting to do this initially complicates the learning process.) Your "pointer," the handgun, should remain pointed (aimed) at your target during the trigger pull. Sounds simple, doesn't it? Point, verify, pull the trigger in a manner that doesn't disturb your "point" and you'll hit the target. The beginner should be effective after as little as 50 rounds of ammo or less. That is, he can "point" or crudely aim the pistol and get good hits at a threat no farther away from him than five yards. (The book *Kill or Get Killed*, by Col. Rex Applegate, is the best reference source for this type of shooting. If there is any single simple method of learning self-defense shooting in a short time period, the Applegate method is it.)

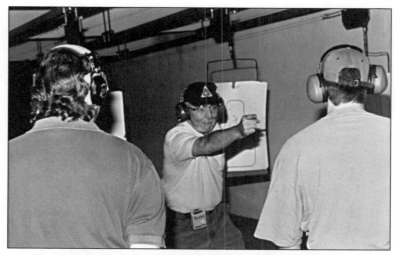

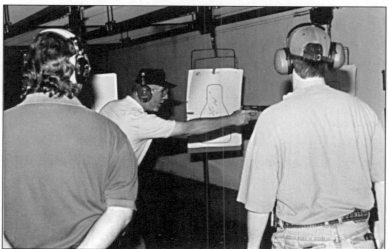

The author, teaching the Applegate point-shooting technique. It is one of the many tools needed to be proficient with personal-defense firearms.

If you're using two hands to grip the gun, as soon as you're hitting where you want to, switch to a one-handed

Joe Venezia and author's wife, point shooting in classic, one-handed Applegate style.

hold and repeat the drill. Next, use the same one-handed hold with the other hand.

When you can get good hits with one hand or two, it's time to shoot from positions other than standing erect, facing the target. Face to the right, face to the left and face to the rear. From each of these positions, engage the target, first with two hands and then with either hand.

Next, get off your feet and onto the ground. Lie on your stomach, your back and your side and shoot. You might well be knocked down during an attack and by doing these drills you will have the knowledge and confidence in your gun handling to be able to keep fighting. Please note, however: Until you are proficient, all these exercises should be done with the gun *already in your hand*. In the case of shooting from the ground, pick the gun up from the ground in front of you. Drawing and reholstering are the most dangerous actions you can do with a loaded gun during practice and should be learned and practiced separately — *with an empty firearm.*

118

One big problem with these suggested drills is that most gun clubs and commercial ranges either tightly control unorthodox practice methods or do not permit them at all. Typically, drawing from a holster and rapidly firing the gun are prohibited for safety reasons. Rolling about on the ground is obviously out, too, because shots fired from ground level may go over the backstop. This isn't much of a drawback, though, for you can "draw" the gun from the shooting bench and reserve holster work for dry-fire exercises at home. And, since the point of any defense work is to be able to accurately and quickly deliver the first shot, rapid firing is not necessarily even a desired skill. In learning defensive pistol work, your *only* goal is to get an effective first shot on the target under any and all conditions.

As you progress with these drills, multiple targets can be used. Put up two, three and then four targets. Now repeat all the drills on the two, then three, then four targets. Ideally, a humanoid target representative of a real threat should be used in practice, but if you're prohibited from doing so, large (at least 8" or 9" diameter) paper plates will do just as well.

Solitary practice can quickly become boring, of course. If you can get a friend who's also interested, it will make your training and

Firing at paper dinner plates is good practice for accuracy and speed.

119

practice more interesting. You can match shots with your friend — who gets the better group? who can pick up and fire the gun more quickly with an accurate first shot? — etc.

The other advantages of a shooting partner (who should have equal or slightly better skills than you, by the way) are that he can watch for your mistakes and point them out to you before you cast them in stone through thousands of repetitions. Also, having someone to motivate you will help you avoid just doing those things that you do well and skipping over the difficult drills.

Before moving on to Chapter 11, I might make one comment on the never-ending debate of point shooting versus aimed shooting, or this-stance versus that-stance. It's an interesting debate, but serves no good purpose in acquiring basic self-defense life-saving skills. In fact, if the debated techniques are used and compared to each other to the exclusion of keeping your primary goal in mind, they serve only to confuse and defeat you in your efforts to acquire the desired skills. Much time can be wasted in

Chris White demonstrates firing a hammerless revolver from his vest pocket at a reactive target.

comparing one-handed, two-handed, point or aimed firing, the isosceles and Weaver stances or anyone else's idea on how to definitively hold and shoot a handgun.

The most important thought in training and practice is to *keep it simple.* This will give you the proficiency to stay alive.

CHAPTER 11

GUNS THAT HAVE WORKED FOR ME

At 59 years of age, I've been carrying a handgun legally — as a Special Agent in the U.S. Army Intelligence Corps; a Special Agent in the U.S. Secret Service; a field investigator with the Warrant Unit, First Judicial District of Philadelphia; an investigator and then Director of Security for a Port of Philadelphia marine terminal; and a private investigator, as well as having held a concealed carry permit since my 18th birthday — for 41 years. As you might imagine, I've developed some pretty concrete opinions on which guns work best for me. When I started out using and evaluating which handgun

The author, shooting a Colt .38 Special revolver with 2" barrel.

was right for me as a self-defense arm there wasn't the plethora of concealed handgun choices that are available now, but good defense guns seem to be timeless.

In the 1950s, no self-respecting TV detective would carry anything other than a 2"-barreled Smith & Wesson or Colt revolver. The few gun magazines of the time all condemned the semi-auto as unreliable and prone to jamming. (Of course, they weren't too far off the mark. Most semi-autos of that era only worked with metal-jacketed, round-nose bullet shapes.) Elmer Keith and Col. Charles Askins, Jr. were the handgun gods and they said the revolver (the S&W was their personal choice) was the only way to go. They weren't wrong then or now. I've used both brands effectively: a Colt Detective Special and an S&W M&P .38 Special revolver — both with 2" barrels. I got the Colt Detective Special first and, sure enough, Keith and Askins were right. The DA stroke was more difficult to use than the S&W, but still manageable. I traded the Colt for the S&W M&P (now Model 10) and found that it did have a better double-action pull; I could hit much better with it. Both concealed well, then and now, and they still shoot the same, too. (I've upgraded the Model 10

Phoenix Armory Model 12 revolver with 2" barrel, for those who want a larger grip, but also concealability.

to a Model 12, customized by Phoenix Armory with a folding spur hammer and slicked-up action, and now a round-butt instead of a square-butt version.)

Also in the 1950s, surplus World War II handguns were as common as dirt. I traded some rifles for a Walther P-38 in 9x19mm, complete with its German Army military holster and spare magazine and also picked up a CZ Model 24 in 9x17mm (.380 auto). I now have the light-weight Walther P-38, a post-WWII-made lightweight version as a house gun and my wife likes the Colt single-action semi-auto .380 Government Model Pocket Lite which, in action type, is similar to the CZ. In as much as

The author's wife, shooting her Colt .380 Government Model Pocket Lite.

the Walther P-38 is the direct ancestor to the S&W semi-autos, S&Ws are also good choices. (And there are still surplus CZs on the market, still as good as ever.)

After a year away at college and a fortuitous friendship with Robert J. Connolly, my 2" S&W went the way of all good guns — traded so that I could buy another gun. Initially, I traded up to the large-frame S&W Model 27 in

.357 Magnum with a 3 ½" barrel. The large-frame S&Ws were (and still are) good shooters, but they're a bit large for good concealment. I also picked up an S&W Model 29 in .44 Magnum with a 5" barrel since Keith and others were touting this as the ultimate self-defense handgun. A .44 Magnum is certainly "enough" gun for most any two-legged creature, but again, it's hard to conceal well (let alone shoot quickly).

Bob Connolly's common sense and his Korean War combat experience while serving in the US Marine Corps finally came to the fore. He got exasperated with me and told me to buy a 1911. I had a false start with the first one, an Ithaca-manufactured GI-surplus British-Lend-Lease 1911A1 .45ACP that cost all of $37.95. It didn't stay around long, for Bob again convinced me that I should trade up for a "real" Colt 1911A1. He was eminently correct and I've carried this very same gun ever since. It's a Commercial Colt 1911A1, serial number 244749-C, that cost me $57.50. I've replaced the barrel and bushing, all the springs and the slide stop. Not bad

Author's original Government Model Commercial 1911-A1, caliber .45ACP, with ivory grips; owned and carried since he was 18!

for nearly 40 years of wear. (It's been reblued three times and was finally given a ROBAR black Teflon finish, as well as being cleaned up and nicely finished by custom gunsmith Joe Bunczk of Phoenix Armory, Norristown, PA, and his associate, Joe Venezia.)

Back in the late 50s, there weren't many gun carriers or hobbyists who favored semi-auto handguns, but the few who did were all 1911 men. The cops and outlaws that I met and knew then mostly went for the .45ACP chambering, but a few of the cops liked the .38 Super because they gained two extra rounds (9) over the .45ACP (7) and found the .38 Super to be a "flatter" shooter, with more penetration than the .45 ACP 230-grain JRN factory ammo.

When I was taking delivery of my Colt 1911, a railroad detective happened to be standing next to me, picking up his new Colt. He looked over and said, "Wrong caliber, son. Use this (the .38 Super); it has more range." I didn't appreciate his advice until a few years later. I was with another railroad detective in a rail yard. He and I both saw some men breaking into a boxcar that was at least a city block away. The detective drew his Colt .38 Super and began shooting at the thieves. He pointed out that the .38 Super's trajectory was so good he didn't have to "hold over" as high to try to get hits. I had my S&W Model 19 loaded with .357 Magnum 110-grain Super Vel-brand jacketed hollow points and got the same results.

Of course, there were a few specialty .45ACP loads available. Winchester offered a 230-grain pointed and jacketed round the company termed "Metal Piercing," with a listed velocity of over 900 feet-per-second. Remington had a competing .45ACP round at 185 grains, the Highway Master, which was pointed, with a 1000-fps advertised velocity. There is nothing much wrong with the .45ACP in 230-grain hardball and the .38 Super with 125-grain Winchester Silvertip +P ammo is a good defensive round.

In this old-time era, there wasn't much done to the 1911 to make it a better carry gun, as is all the rage today. Curiously, the guns worked just fine with GI hardball ammo and if they were kept clean, they didn't jam. The people who got shot with the big-bore gun died without protesting the lack of an effective hollowpoint bullet for the .45ACP.

I was fortunate to become associated with some interesting gun handlers during my college years and we did some tinkering with the 1911. J. Woodrow (Woody) Mathews, Jr. decided that, since he carried the 1911 loaded with the hammer down, an extended hammer spur was the way to go. He enlisted the aid of Peter J. Seitz and Everett Spear to weld up a hammer spur extension ala a single-action Colt revolver. This worked for Woody, but the hammer spur caught in coat linings and the idea was abandoned.

Pete Seitz and Everett Spear were both students at the Pennsylvania Gunsmithing School in Pittsburgh, PA, so they had the facilities to experiment and herein lies one of life's great missed opportunities.

Collectively, we saw that since the 1911 worked best cocked and locked, the safety really needed to be a tad bigger. Pete and Everett made up half a dozen extended thumb safeties for us. They worked just fine, but we thought they stuck out too much to fit in the then-available holsters and, in my case, the safety went into a parts box. (I still have two of the originals.) We all figured no one would ever want an extended thumb safety on a

1911. Hah! The extended tactical safety is now almost *mandatory* for any 1911 carried for self-defense.

When military service came along, all the guns got greased up and stored away, for Uncle Sam had his own ideas on "which is the right gun for you." I enlisted in the U.S. Army Intelligence Corps (CIC) as a Special Agent and, lo and behold, I was right back where I started — with an issued 2" Colt Detective Special. Nothing changed. I still couldn't shoot the Colt well and my issue gun was so out of time that it misfired more often than not, so in 1963 I got one of the new S&W Model 19s in .357 Magnum with a 4" barrel. Bill Jordan had put his mark of approval on this model, named the Combat Magnum. I think it cost somewhere in the neighborhood of $90. This was another good investment, for I went on to carry it in other jobs, still have it and it still performs well. The modern gun toter can still get this S&W with a 2 ½" or 4" barrel in blue (Model 19) or stainless (Model 66) versions and be well-armed.

After being appointed a Special Agent with the U.S. Secret Service, I was issued an S&W Model 15 .38 Special with a 4" barrel. It didn't take very long before I substituted my personal Model 19 for the issue .38. In a holster (Bucheimer was issue, as I recall), with similar grips, no one was the wiser.

I also used the M19 when I was an investigator on the Philadelphia waterfront, only giving it up, as well as my 1911, for an S&W Model 59, caliber 9x19mm, when it came on the market. On the waterfront, the S&W Model 59 with 14 rounds in the mag and two spares made a lot of sense!

Of course, over all this time, there were experiments with

other concealment handguns. I must have owned at least seven Walther PP-series guns, both the PP and the PPK models. They were fine back-up or off-duty guns, but I never quite got the hang of them. I traded the last of them off for an S&W Model 36 five-shot revolver and then the same gun in stainless steel, the Model 60. (Now, for a

deep-concealment semi-auto, I use a Phoenix Armory-customized Russian Makarov chambered for the 9x18 Makarov round. I think the Russians have an excellent, updated version of the Walther PP guns.)

This particular handgun, the Makarov in 9x18mm, is extremely reliable. This one has been improved even more with light modifications by Phoenix Armory.

The little five-shooters are the quintessential pocket or concealment gun. Once I discovered S&W's Model 40 and 42, the hammerless versions of the Model 36, I retired my M60. I've been using both the S&W Model 42 (the Airweight version) and the Model 40 (the all-steel version) since as both primary and back-up guns. Smith now offers this model in stainless steel and also cham-

Smith & Wesson Models 40 (top) and 42 in .38 Special are two of the author's favorite light-duty guns.

Author's Browning .25 was his deep-cover back-up gun for many years.

bered for the 9x19mm (Luger) and .357 Magnum cartridges.

Two other guns I liked then and now are the original Colt (pre-WWII vintage) Pocket Auto, chambered in .25ACP, and the Baby Browning .25 auto. Until Louis and Leander Seecamp invented their great Seecamp DA-only .32ACP pocket auto, the Colt or Browning .25 was my constant companion. They truly were "go anywhere" guns and are very good as unobtrusive back-up or deep-conceal-ment hand-guns. The Colt is, unfortunate-ly, long gone and the Browning hon-orably retired, replaced by the Seecamp .32.

The Seecamp .32 replaced the Browning .25.

I replaced the S&W M59 with a Browning High Power in 9x19mm (replacing one I had traded away while a Secret Service Agent). This gun is now a full-house custom piece done by Richard Heinie. Another HP, originally bought as a spare, is now a Wayne Novak "One of One Hundred" custom gun.

In 1980, I had the good fortune to meet the late Armand Swenson, a master pistolsmith on the 1911. He took a liking to me and I was able to get a "Swenson" in less

than the normal five-year delivery time (the original customer died while waiting for the gun) and I still occasionally use it, as well as a second Swenson 1911, along with my original commercial Colt as daily-carry handguns.

Heinie- (top) and Novak-customized Browning High Powers; fine examples of the art of these pistolsmiths.

Dick Heinie and other excellent custom 'smiths such as Jim Garthwaite, Mike LaRocca and Bill Laughridge have built lightweight

Armand Swenson built this .45ACP semi-auto for the author in 1982, and it still gives good service.

Colt Commanders, an Officers' ACP, a 10mm Colt Delta Elite and a Para-Ordnance 13-round 1911 for me. They're all great for self-defense and they should be, for they represent the state-of-the-art in fit, finish and function in the gunmaker's art of customizing the Colt 1911. Problem is, they're all so damned nice that I hate to carry them (though I do), knowing that I could easily wind up without one of them if I had need to use it in self-defense.

Since Gaston Glock stunned the gun world with his new and truly innovative "Safe Action" semi-auto pistols, I've found myself using one of the Glock guns on a frequent basis. They're sure not the prettiest guns in the world and they don't take to much custom work, but they're always reliable and durable.

Glock Model 20 in 10mm.

Forty-plus years of gun carrying in law enforcement and private life and my choices boil down to the Colt 1911, the Browning High Power, some model of a Glock pistol (preferably a 10mm or .45ACP), a Makarov (9x18mm), any of the J-frame S&W .38 Special revolvers, the S&W Model 12 with 2" barrel and a .32ACP Seecamp, with the S&W Model 19 .357 Mag thrown in for good measure.

I don't make any claims that these are the best guns for everyone, but they have stood the test of time for me. Sure, there are ten times as many other models and flavors of handguns out there that may "fit" someone else much better than my choices, but these work for me.

You'll note that I haven't gotten into the cartridge/bullet design debate. I'm only comfortable with ammunition that will feed *100% of the time* in semi-autos, which means either a round-nose Full Metal Jacket bullet or a Hollow Point bullet whose shape mimics the FMJ round.

Reliability and bullet placement are the **only** criteria for a self-defense arm. In revolvers, any of the brand-name manufacturers' Jacketed Hollow Point or lead semi-wad-cutter ammo is good. In the deep concealment guns, I use only the FMJ design. I'll leave the design debate and analysis to others.

CHAPTER 12

TRAVEL SMART, TRAVEL SAFE

Going on vacation? Getting away from the daily grind of the job, the bosses and the everyday frustrations of life? Going to have fun in the sun? Kick back and relax? Sounds good. However, there are a few things you need to do before, during and after this hopefully-idyllic vacation.

In essence, let's not leave our common sense behind when we take off for the airport or hit the open road. (To borrow a line from a famous commercial "...don't leave home without it.") First, prepare your house for the trip. No, it's not going with you, but you also don't want its contents traveling with someone else while you're gone.

Preparations are fairly simple. Discontinue your daily newspaper — but don't tell them it's only for vacation. Ideally, if you can arrange to have a live-in house sitter (someone you already know and trust, of course; this is not the time to try out new help), you will be in really good shape. He or she can continue with the daily paper, answer the phone, get the mail that's stuffed in the mail box, mow the lawn, answer the door for any deliveries or inquiries plus move your car(s) around (if not parked in a garage). If you haven't noticed, a car sitting for a week has debris and leaves piled up under and against the

Leaves and other debris around a parked car's tires are a sure clue that it hasn't been moved for awhile. So if you're away from home for any length of time, arrange to have your car moved periodically.

tires, showing no movement. Also, the house sitter should have a random schedule while staying in your home.

If you have valuables, put them in your bank safe deposit box. If you have firearms, they should already be in a safe but, in addition, disassemble them and put the operating pieces in different locations. Home security safes can be opened just like any other iron box, and what thief wants part of a gun?

Light timers are nice, inside and out, but only if they're random on and off. Leaving the outside lights on 24 hours a day is the same as hanging out a sign announcing, "Nobody Home!" It is also a very smart idea to notify your local police that you'll be gone and that there will be someone else in your home. The house sitter will not appreciate being held at gun point if your neighbors call the cops when they see a stranger going into your house. Speaking of neighbors, if you get along with them and they're responsible, let them know your arrangements and, if possible, introduce the house sitter to them.

OK, the house is set up and you've given the house sitter your travel itinerary, including locations and phone numbers of hotels. If worse comes to worst, and you do have some misfortune while traveling and don't come back when scheduled, your house sitter can give the authorities some idea of where to start looking for you. I realize this is a bit morbid, but it's reality.

OK, you've made it into the airplane or you've gotten a few hours along on the interstate. You did call ahead and make confirmed reservations for the night didn't you? It's not too smart to be wandering in and out of hotels in strange towns in the dark looking for a room. It's all too easy to make a wrong turn and find out exactly where the gang bangers and the crack dealers hang out. If, when you arrive at your chosen hotel and it isn't up to your standards, use the lobby phone and the telephone directory to find something more suitable.

I don't stay in motels where the desk clerk works behind bullet-resistant Lexan. I also make it a point to look at the surrounding area. One motel my wife and I checked into in upstate New York was adequate, but our room overlooked a very large junkyard and a heavily-wooded area. I asked for another room more centrally located. They said they had nothing else, so we left. (It was early in the afternoon, so we had plenty of time to safely find another motel.)

If the back or the side of your motel looks like this — move on!

While on the road, if you have a break down, follow all the rules that have been repeated over and over again. If you have a cell phone, call for assistance. If a non-uniformed stranger offers help, keep the doors locked and

Great items for self-defense when disabled on the road — a Glock Entrenching Tool (a shovel) and road flares. They're legal everywhere!

decline his help other than to ask him to call the police for you. (You can make your own decision to go along with his offer, but you're gambling.) If you have road flares that you put out to signal your breakdown, keep a few unlit ones to use as a "deterrent" if necessary. This would go for your tire iron, too. But, don't be foolhardy. I know of one case where a middle-aged man got out of his car (rather than driving away) with a baseball bat to confront a gang of teenagers. They beat him to death! He was outmatched right from the start.

Conversely, another man, 72-years-young, turned into a suburban side street one block from his home when a gang of youths blocked his way at the intersection. They yelled "go around, old man." He drove his 1963 Chrysler 300 right through them and then drove over neighbors' lawns, chasing them with the car. (This was overkill, of course, but I didn't argue with my father. He just asked me to go arrange to repair the lawns and have a few words with the gang on the corner.)

As far as self-protection goes when you travel, taking a gun along is sometimes quite awkward and illegal to boot. If you choose to take a handgun with you while flying you must always go through the checked baggage routine, for Federal law doesn't allow civilians to carry *any* firearm into the passenger cabin. There are regulations against carrying firearms on trains or buses, too. However, in the absence of metal detectors, it would appear that you can at least secure the gun in your carry bag. If you are driving, you can pack whatever will fit in the car, but be aware that some states mandate that the gun be unloaded, with ammunition separate, and that both be locked up and unaccessible to the driver. Some states allow open, unconcealed carry, others permit a gun in the glove box. The NRA is an excellent source for the specifics of various state laws.

One of the absurdities of concealed-carry laws is that where you probably will need a gun the most, you are most often not permitted to have a loaded gun anywhere near you. You most certainly cannot have a gun permit in all 50 states, because even if you could meet the various states' gun permit requirements, not all states grant carry permits to their residents, let alone non-residents. On a positive note, with the exception of a few

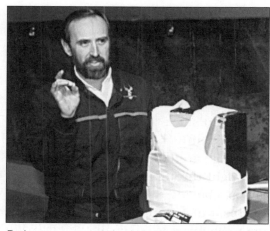

Body armor can and should be worn in high-threat areas, even if you cannot be armed. (Here, Safariland body armor is being demonstrated by Tom Campbell.)

states, you are "allowed" to have a loaded gun inside your "temporary" residence, be it a motel, hotel or private home. It leaves a gray area if you're in a mobile camper or RV, though. If it's moving, it's considered to be a car; if it's parked, it's a "home" in some states.

Of course, if you choose to break the law by taking and/or carrying "old Betsy" with you, you may be committing a felony, or at the very least a misdemeanor. The police are not inclined to turn a blind eye toward you just because you're such a nice, law-abiding citizen since, in fact, you're not — you're breaking their laws.

Just remember — the bad guys aren't on vacation. If you choose to travel unarmed, that's where you stay in your locked car and wait for the police or AAA to arrive. AAA is a wise addition to your bag of safety tricks, by the way, if you're not already a member. Not only do you get safe, usually-timely road assistance, but you can count on the AAA Travel Guides to point you to quality accommodations. (My wife and I have found the AAA motel rating system to be pretty accurate most of the time.)

If you think you're being followed while driving, there's a quick way to find out. Make four right or left turns. If the car's still behind you, it's following you. Drive to a brightly-lit convenience store and call the police. Forget trying to find a police station; their locations aren't well marked and they may be closed at night, particularly in very small communities. Of course, If you see a police car by the side of the road, stop a good distance behind him and flash your lights and blow the horn. If he's going the other way, do the same thing. He'll notice you more often than not, even going in the opposite direction. And don't be embarrassed about a possible false alarm. Your instincts are probably good and the officer will be attentive. Bad guys don't give off too many signals of their intent and the officer knows this much better than you.

Of course, you don't need to just "hope for the best" if you leave your firearms at home. You can and should avail yourself of some tools that could help tip the scales in your favor if the need arises.

First off, any blunt object is better than using your hands and feet, despite the action scenes in martial arts movies. Your choice of the blunt object is limited only by your imagination. A single heavy book or bag full of books, your stuffed briefcase, a portable personal computer, your traveling luggage — all are blunt instruments to use in self-defense. One friend of mine "suitcased" a mugger and he said it works well. As he was going to get his rental car at an airport, a guy ran up behind him and my friend swung his two-suiter back into the guy's knees, knocking him down. Now, my friend has had three tours in the U.S. Marine Corps in Vietnam, has five Purple Hearts and the Silver Star, so he's not the type to just leave things alone. He, of course, turned and finished the job with his feet before going on to pick up his rental car.

Moving up from the standard blunt object that no one would ever classify as a weapon, there are hiking sticks, canes and umbrellas. Any of these are better than the blunt object because they increase your reach and your defense options. The walking stick, cane and umbrella are just modern versions of a caveman's stick or club. Another friend of mine, crippled by polio, needs a cane to walk. He's also become a master at stick fighting.

If you think that carrying a cane without any visible signs of infirmity would be a bit too dandified, you can carry an umbrella most places. (Although it certainly would be out of place in areas like the sunny Southwest.) An umbrella is no more than a weak cane that can have a hooked handle and a very pointed end. (Skip the sword canes and umbrellas, though, or you're right back there breaking the law on carrying a concealed deadly weapon, so you might as well be carrying a handgun.)

But remember, umbrellas and canes are to poke and hook with, not to use like the archetypical little old lady who beats someone about the head with it. Of course, an umbrella can be strengthened by the addition of a metal bar and then used as a bludgeon, but you're back to where this sure looks like a prohibited, albeit makeshift, weapon.

Speaking of metal bars, one of my security guards at a marine terminal on the Philadelphia waterfront had a habit of always wearing wrist-covering work gloves and long-sleeved jackets. He was 73 years old and still working security unarmed (as required by management). I noticed his habit and finally asked Florian why he dressed the way he did. The old Polish gentleman, a long-retired Philadelphia Police officer, grinned at me with a twinkle in his eyes and raised his coat sleeve to show me a foot-long flat bar of steel up his sleeve. If he needed to, he merely swatted his threat with his arm of steel.

The point is, there are many everyday items and tools that can be used defensively. Even a simple ball point pen or a #2 sharpened wood pencil can work. I've carried both when doing interviews within the open "population" of prisons. Walking totally unarmed among long-term, convicted felons is not everyone's cup of tea — certainly not mine. Can I survive with a pen or a pencil? Probably not, but at least I'll go down fighting with the pencil or pen firmly imbedded in someone's eye socket.

Speaking of prisons, many correctional officers use a simple, improvised flail — their jailhouse keys on a key ring attached to their belts with a long, leather, quick-release strap. When they have trouble, they

For women, who aren't as likely to carry their keys on a leather strap, the double-pointed "Lady Finger" brass key ring can be a helpful self-defense tool.

unsnap the key ring and use it just like a medieval flail. You can do the very same thing with your car and house keys and it's perfectly legal in any airport or public buildings that prohibit weapons. Used this way, the keys are much more effective than the usual advice of jabbing someone with the keys stuck between your fingers. Flailing away is a gross body motor movement as opposed to trying to remember to insert the keys correctly into your fingers.

Carrying a knife is another matter entirely. Authorities are not going to look at a Swiss army knife as a weapon; the same authorities are going to lock you up if you're toting your Randell-made fighting Bowie. The Randell is much better for

Carrying a Swiss Army knife, left, is permissible. The Bowie knife on the right (circa 1850s) is not.

the job, but the Swiss army knife, particularly one with a locking blade, will afford you some measure of defense.

The biggest problem with a knife is that 99.9% of the people carrying them aren't going to stab or cut anyone. It's foreign to most all of our training and upbringing to assault someone with a knife. (It should be noted, though, that this doesn't apply to criminals, many of whom are extremely-proficient knife users.)

The knife is an excellent close-range weapon. It never jams and never runs out of ammunition. Up close, at grappling distances, it can be quicker and more deadly than a handgun round. If you want to carry a knife, I'd suggest a decent-sized locking Swiss Army knife, one of the small folding knives that have an "easy-open" feature or a very ordinary fixed-blade hunting or fishing knife. Skip the bayonets, daggers and fancy folders. Particularly if you're traveling on airlines; the Swiss Army knife will "pass," but some other folding knives won't.

Pepper sprays are most often the recommended less-than-lethal defense tool. They do work, but not all the time and, curiously, pepper and tear gas sprays are prohibited weapons in a number of areas of the world. Hair spray, oven cleaner, gun scrubbers or brake and carborator cleaners are not, however, and all will cause discomfort, if not permanent damage, if sprayed into an attacker's eyes.

Pepper spray is prohibited in many areas; oven cleaner is not!

Any of the aerosol sprays are prohibited by the airlines in both your stowed or carry-on luggage because the containers can discharge or explode due to altitude-induced air pressure changes. The upside is that all these same items are readily available at your destination.

You can also carry a bright flashlight such as a SureFire or Streamlight. The bright mini-lights are good two ways: for the bright blinding light and as an impact tool. Using both features, coupled with the application of a defensive spray of some sort might give you time to get away from the problem. But, again, *you* have to make the choices.

Of course, the improvised device you select for defense should not look like nor be carried like a weapon. Your chosen tool should be able to withstand the court's scrutiny as it decides if you intended your tool to be a weapon or you just "happened" to use it as one in self-defense.

You should always keep road flares in your car in case it breaks down. They can be used to your advantage, yet they aren't considered to be "weapons."

Now, as far as just plain fighting — and you could well be an umpteenth-degree black belt in whatever — if you anticipate a bare-handed fight, why on earth would you wear soft shoes such as sneakers or their variants? A good, sturdy pair of low quarters with sharp-edged soles or a pair of tough, well-made hiking boots are much better to use to deliver effective kicks. Your opponent is supposed to have the broken bones, not you. In my various law enforcement and security jobs, I have always opted for some sort of dress boot rather than low shoes for this very reason. The boot also offers more protection to you if you're attacked.

As far as other clothing worn while traveling, it should be comfortable enough to run or fight in but not noticeable enough to attract attention. Leave the Rolex watch and diamond rings at home or in your carry-on travel bag and wear a Timex. A leather overcoat may be the height of fashion, but it's also a damned good lure for a predator. (Although a *subdued* leather jacket is excellent protection against knives and punches.)

Also, you should dress to blend in with your surroundings. In other words, regionalize your dress. If you're in the Northeastern United States, a business suit, loafers, topcoat, dress hat, white shirt and tie fit the bill. If you're going to rural America, of course, the same clothing would make you stand out like a circus freak.

When traveling overnight, I would advise you to stay in the best hotels that you can afford. And, of course, you should stay with the mainstream folks and not get a cheap room at a motel that rents by the hour!

Once you're at the rental desk, it's a good idea to get a room that is not above the fourth or fifth floor. Most fire truck ladders can't reach much higher than that. I would also avoid a ground floor room, particularly if the room opens right into the parking lot, unless you want to be as close as possible to your car if it's alarmed. If you've got a rental car, take extra insurance and leave the car-theft problem to the rental company, the insurer and the cops.

Once you get to your room, take note of the fire exits and then look at your motel room door. Don't just go up to it, use the key and enter. Look at the door. I was about to stay at one motel in the Quantico, Virginia-area when I noticed that there were pry marks on both the inside and the outside of the door. I don't know why the marks were there or what they were from, but I left and got another room in another motel.

Once in your room, check to see how the door and windows secure. The chain lock is useless; only deadbolts work. The window and adjoining room doors should be well-secured; otherwise get another room. It's not only in the movies that burglars make entry through motel room windows. And don't dismiss any window as being too small to get through. Burglars come in all sizes and shapes and are also known to use children to gain entrance.

Once you've settled in, know who you're opening the door for. If someone knocks and announces maid service, don't just pop the door open without at least looking out to see if it really is the maid. Of course, this should be in the morning or early afternoon hours. I've never found maids working at midnight. And if you didn't order towels or room service, I'd decline the offer — day or night. If you do have doubts about whoever's outside the door, call the front desk or the police. You can also just leave if you have an alternative exit. Do the windows open at all? If you had to, could you make it down from your room to the ground?

Some hotels have a policy of calling you first before sending employees to your room. It doesn't hurt to call back to see if it was, in fact, someone from the front desk who called.

One time when my wife and I were in Caracas, Venezuela, our room was called by a person who said he was the "front desk" and asked if the porter could be admitted to restock the bottled water. I agreed and immediately there was a knock at the door. I figured this was much too quick; I had just hung up the phone. I looked out and the person standing there appeared to be a genuine hotel employee, compete with uniform. I still opened the door with a cocked and locked 1911 .45ACP pointed directly at the gentleman. (We were in Venezuela for a World Practical Shooting match.) He wasn't disturbed in the least. He entered, restocked the water and left. I guess this wasn't an uncommon occurrence for him.

I might add that this expensive hotel had uniformed police stationed in the lobby and roaming the upper floors armed with UZI submachine guns and wearing Level IV body armor. I figured that they knew more than I did about the criminal activity at the hotel, hence the gun greeting at our door. By the way, as the porter left the room I saw why he was so quick. He was wearing a portable two-way radio and I surmised that the front desk told him to knock as soon as they received an OK from the room's occupant.

Another point. Try to restrain yourself from making friends with everyone you meet at the bar, the pool and the restaurant. There are those professionals who look for just such behavior and take advantage of your lack of common sense. Curiously, folks who are the most reserved at home, seem to go out of their way to be exactly the opposite on vacation. They want to talk to everyone. Next thing you know, everyone is sharing a cab or a convenient rental car to go to an interesting tourist site or restaurant. Skip the cheap ride and have the hotel call a cab or use your own car. You want to get to where you're going and not visit (permanently) a roadside ditch. (And, by the way, go to *good* restaurants or bars. The food and drinks cost more, but you probably won't have to fight your way out.)

If you do strike up casual acquaintances, keep the socializing to open, occupied areas. Don't invite strangers to your motel room or got to theirs. Of course, hospitality suites are fine if they're listed on the hotel directory. Go there and leave in a group. Know where the escape routes are. This not only includes the normal fire exits (which it doesn't hurt to use at least once), but can you get out of where you are other than through the main door? Often in suites, the side door to the adjoining room is open and you can slip out this way. (You *have* checked this same door in your own room to make sure it's locked, haven't you?)

When you leave your room in the evening, keep the TV and the lights on. When you come back, everything should be as you left it. After opening the door, push it completely open and look to see that there's no one in the room (just as you should have done when first renting and entering the room). Start from the bathroom area to · the other side of the beds. I've had desk clerks mess up on who got what keys more than once. One time, I had someone attempt to come into my room after I was already in bed. (He had been checked in and given a key to my room at the front desk.) Another time, I got "my" key to "my" room and when I opened the door, the room was already occupied. (Another reason to double-lock the door when you're in the room, even during the day.)

Since many of us are firearms and self-defense oriented, we often have occasion to have firearms with us for competition or hunting. As I mentioned earlier, most states consider your motel room your "home" and you can legally have a firearm with you. Just keep the gun and the shells handy but separate, and secure them and anything else gun-related so that the maids and other support staff will not see or handle them as they clean the room. This may well entail you carrying the guns back and forth to your car whenever you go out. In my handgun competition circles, the shooters will sometimes even carry their properly-secured handguns into restaurants rather than leaving them in the car. That's just the inconvenient cost of being careful of your possessions and being responsible about firearms safety.

Okay. Vacation's over and you're on your way home. You still need to observe the same travel rules — and do call ahead to your house sitter. You don't want to startle him. If he's not there, call a friend to go to your house to check it out. You don't want to have done all this good, preventive security work just to come home and walk into a trap.

The bottom line of all this? *Always pay attention to your surroundings.* At home as well as while traveling, shopping or just goofing off. When you enter or leave a building, when you're walking or driving or shopping or just sitting in a park — look around. Notice who and what are nearby. In plain words...get your head out of your butt!

Always be aware of your surroundings, no matter how innocent they may look. Parking lots in busy shopping areas may appear "safe," but can be the scene of violent encounters.

Trust yourself and your instincts. If something or someone doesn't look "right," it or the person probably isn't. Avoid what disturbs you. A few minutes of inconvenience to be right sure beats an eternity to be wrong.

POSTSCRIPT

Your survival in the face of an actual or threatened assault against you or your loved ones brings you to one terrible but unequivocal truth. You may be forced to take another man's life. To survive, you must come to terms with an act that goes against all of your upbringing and cherished values.

Many very eloquent, articulate and educated writers in the field of self-defense and survival skills use any number of euphemisms to address the subject of killing. They talk of "deterrence," "avoidance," "stopping the attack," "surviving the attack" and, of course, "self-defense." They don't just plainly say that sometimes you may need to kill to live. Most talk about "stopping" or "neutralizing" a person they call a "goblin" or a "threat" or an "adversary," but never identify him as someone who is going to rob you of your most precious possession — your life or the lives of your loved ones.

For a normal, law-abiding, moral person to kill another human being is totally abhorrent and it is, quite possibly, impossible for some to do. You cannot and will not know what you will do if the occasion should arise. You can think you will — or you can think you will not — kill. But mark this well: if you do take a life, you will be forever changed by that life-taking.

I cannot advise you as to your choice. You can read on the matter. You can talk to a religious leader of your choice, a doctor or a psychiatrist. They may well be able to help you come to terms with your concerns, but they cannot make the decision for you. It is your responsibility alone and you will live — or die — with it. I will only say that in a final, life-threatening conflict, if you are to live, Otherhuman must die, *for he does not have the right or privilege to harm you!*

If you ever have to confront Otherhuman, always keep in mind that he does not have the right to harm you or your family!

BIBLIOGRAPHY

Applegate, Col. Rex, *Kill or Get Killed*. Paladin Press, Boulder, CO/1976.

Ayoob, Massad, *The Truth About Self-Protection*. Bantam Books, Inc., New York, NY/1993.

Jordan, William H., *No Second Place Winner*. W.H. Jordan, Shreveport, LA/1965.

Keith, Elmer, *Sixguns*. The Stackpole Company, Harrisburg, PA/1955; Wolfe Publishing Co., Prescott, AZ/1992.

Keith, Elmer, *Hell, I Was There!* Petersen Publishing Co., Los Angeles, CA/1979.

McGivern, Ed, *Fast and Fancy Revolver Shooting*. New Win Publishing, Inc., Clinton, NJ/1975, 1984.

Nichols, Bob, *The Secrets of Double-Action Shooting*. G.P. Putnam's Sons, New York, NY/1950.

The Philadelphia Inquirer, "A New Generation of Killers, Feeling No Blame and No Shame." Philadelphia Newspapers, Inc., Philadelphia, PA/12-6-92.

About the author....

Upon receiving his BS degree from Carnegie Tech and completing service as a Special Agent in U.S. Army Intelligence, Walt Rauch was a Special Agent with the U.S. Secret Service and an Investigator with the Philadelphia (PA) Fugitive Squad (where he made over 2,000 felony arrests). He now operates his own investigative and security consulting company, Rauch & Company, Ltd., as well as the Advanced Tactical Group, Ltd. (ATG), a research, development and training group for defense, weapons and tactics. Detective agency services include investigations in both criminal and civil matters, process service and expert witness testimony on firearms use and tactics.

Rauch is also a writer and lecturer in the firearms field. He is published regularly in national and international publications including *Combat Handguns, Guns & Weapons for Law Enforcement* and other Harris Publications specialty magazines, the NRA's *American Guardian, Police & Security News, Cibles* (France) and *Visier* (Germany).

Use this form to order additional copies
of *REAL-WORLD SURVIVAL!*

NAME_____

ADDRESS _____

CITY_____ STATE_____ ZIP_____

Number of copies @ $15.95 ea.   _____

Shipping & Handling @ $4 ea.   _____

Sales tax, if applicable*   _____

Total amount enclosed   _____

*PA shipping address must include 6% sales tax

Send check or money order to:

RAUCH & COMPANY, LTD.
P.O. Box 510
Lafayette Hill, PA 19444

Prices valid in the USA only
All orders subject to availability
Volume pricing available; contact
publisher for details.
Please allow 4-6 weeks for delivery